The Great Musicians

Rossini and His School

H. Sutherland Edwards

TABLE OF CONTENTS

CHAPTER I

ROSSINI'S CHILDHOOD AND YOUTH

A CONTEMPORARY of Cimarosa and of Paisiello, his predecessors, but not, except at the very outset of his career, his models, and of Donizetti, Bellini, and Verdi, his successors, and in an artistic sense his followers, Rossini is a central figure in the nineteenth-century history of Italian music.

Lives of Rossini have been published freely enough during the last fifty or sixty years. It but rarely happens, even to the greatest man, to have his biography written or his statue erected during his lifetime. But Rossini lived so long that it seemed impossible to wait for his death; and more than one writer seized upon him when he was still a young man. Perhaps it occurred to the Abbé Carpani, the first of Rossini's biographers, that he was already approaching the critical age at which so many great composers— not to speak of painters and poets—had ceased not only to work but to live; Mozart, for instance, Cimarosa, Weber, Hérold, Bellini, Schubert, and Mendelssohn. It has been suggested, indeed, that Rossini might perhaps have wished his career to be measured against those of so many other composers whose days were cut short at about the age he had attained when he produced William Tell. Rossini was but thirty-seven when William Tell, his last work for the stage, and his last work of any importance with the exception of the Stabat Mater was brought out. But when, soon after the production of Semiramide, played for the first time in 1823, Stendhal published that Life of Rossini which is known to be founded almost entirely on the Abbé Carpani's work, Rossini, at the age of thirty-one, had already completed the most important portion of his artistic life. Readable, interesting, and in many places charming, Stendhal's Life of Rossini is at the same time meagre, and, worse still, untrustworthy. But there is no reason why a tolerable Life of Rossini, including an account of all the changes and reforms introduced by this composer into Italian opera, should not have been published when he was only thirty-one years of age. There would have been nothing of moment to add to it but a narrative of Rossini's visit to London, of his residence in Paris, and above all, of the circumstances under which he produced William Tell together with his reasons—if they could only be discovered—for abandoning composition when he had once produced that work.

The life of Rossini divides itself, more naturally than most things to which this favourite mode of division is applied, into three parts. During the first period of his existence, extending from his birth to the year 1823 when Semiramide was brought out, he made his reputation. From 1823 when he visited London and Paris, until 1829 when he produced his great masterpiece in the serious style, and afterwards threw down his pen for ever, he made his fortune. Finally, from 1829, the year of William Tell, until 1869, the year of his death, he enjoyed his fortune and his reputation; caring not too much for either, and so little desirous to increase the former that he abandoned his "author's rights" in France—fees, that is to say, which he was entitled to receive for the representation of his works—to the Society of Musical Composers.

Rossini made his appearance in public when he was only seven years of age; doing so not, it need scarcely be said, in the character of a composer, but in that of a singer. It was in Paer's Camilla, composed for Vienna and afterwards brought out at Bologna, that Rossini, in the year 1799, took the part of a child. "Nothing," says Madame Giorgi-Righetti, the original Rosina in the Barber of Seville,[1] "could be more tender, more touching, than the voice and action of this extraordinary child in the beautiful canon of the third act; senti si fiero instante. The Bolognese of that time declared that he would some day be one of the greatest musicians known. I need not say whether the prophecy has been verified."

Gioachino Antonio Rossini was born on the 29th February, 1792; and the circumstance of his having come into the world in a leap-year justified him, he used to maintain, in counting his birthday, not annually according to the usual custom, but once every four years. According to this method of computation he had numbered nineteen birthdays when, at the age of seventy-seven, he died. What is better worth remembering is the fact that Rossini was born, as if by way of compensation, the very year in which Mozart died; Mozart who, indebted to the Italians for much of the sweetness and singableness of his lovely melodies, was to give to Italy, through Rossini, new instrumental combinations, new dramatic methods, and new operatic forms.

It may have been very desirable to show that Rossini was of distinguished ancestry, and that he had a great-uncle, who, in the middle of the sixteenth century, was governor of Ravenna.

---

[1] Cenni di una donna già cantante sopra il maestro Rossini.

But it is more interesting to know that he was of good musical parentage. His father, it is true, was nothing more than town trumpeter at Pesaro; herald and crier, that is to say, to the sound of the trumpet. But his mother was what musicians call "an artist." She possessed a very beautiful voice; and when the town trumpeter fell ill or in some other manner incapacitated himself for supporting the family, she replaced him as bread-winner by taking an engagement as an operatic singer. According to one of Rossini's biographers, Rossini the trumpeter came to grief through his political opinions, which were of a more decided character than any that were ever professed, publicly at least, by his eminent son. When, after the Italian campaign, the French army in 1796 entered Pesaro, the old Rossini so far forgot his official position and the duty he owed to the state, as to proclaim his sympathy and admiration for the Republican troops; on whose retirement he was punished for his want of loyalty, being first deprived of his employment and afterwards cast into prison.

The trumpet was not the only instrument cultivated by the elder Rossini. He also played the horn; playing it, not like an ordinary town crier, from whom only a few loud flourishes would be expected by way of preliminary announcement, but in true musicianly style.

The horn, eighty years ago, was not a very important instrument in Italian orchestration. But such as it was the elder Rossini played it in more than one operatic band; and in due time, and to all appearances as soon as it was physically possible to do so, the father taught the art of playing the horn to his precocious son. Rossini was still very young when he accompanied his parents on musical excursions, or "tours" as they would now be called; and on these occasions, when the father took the part of first horn in some local orchestra—which was sometimes nothing more than the band of a travelling show—the part of second horn was assigned to the son. The mother at the same time sang on the stage. Rossini, then, at once vocalist and instrumentalist, began his career in both characters at a very early age. It has been seen that at seven he appeared on the stage as an operatic singer. Between the ages of seven and twelve he was much occupied in horn playing; and his performances in company with his father had probably some effect in developing that taste for wind instruments and especially for horns, for which his orchestration was one day to be remarkable.

In his thirteenth year Rossini was taken to Bologna and presented to Professor Tesci of that city. The professor heard the little boy sing and play, and was so pleased with his performances that he procured him an engagement as chorister in one of the local churches. It was of this period in Rossini's life that Heine was thinking when, in his well-known article on Rossini's Stabat Mater, he wrote: "The true character of Christian art does not reside in thinness and plainness of the body, but in a certain effervescence of the soul which neither the musician nor the painter can appropriate to himself either by baptism or by study; and in this respect I find in the Stabat of Rossini a more truly Christian character than in the Paulus of Felix Mendelssohn Bartholdy; an oratorio which the adversaries of Rossini point to as a model of the Christian style. Heaven preserve me from wishing to express by that the least blame against a master so full of merits as the composer of Paulus; and the author of these letters is less likely than any one to wish to criticise the Christian character of the oratorio in question from clerical, or, so to say, pharisaical reasons. I cannot, however, avoid pointing out that at the age when Mendelssohn commenced Christianity at Berlin (he was only baptized in his thirteenth year), Rossini had already deserted it a little, and had lost himself entirely in the mundane music of operas. Now he has again abandoned the latter to carry himself back in dreams to the Catholic recollections of his first youth—to the days when he sang as a child in the choir of the Pesaro [for which read Bologna] cathedral, and took part as an acolyte in the service of the holy mass."

Besides enabling him to earn money by singing in the churches, Professor Tesci gave his young friend lessons in singing and pianoforte playing, so that after two years he could execute the most difficult music at first sight. He now was found competent to act as musical director, and accepted an engagement in that character with a travelling company which gave performances at various little towns in the Romagna. When he was fifteen years of age Rossini gave up his engagement as director to the wandering troop and went back to Bologna, where (1807) he was admitted as a student to the Lyceum. Such application and such intelligence did he now show, that after he had been but one year at the academy he was chosen by the director, Professor Mattei, to compose the cantata expected annually from the Lyceum's best pupil.

Rossini's first work, written when he was sixteen years of age and executed at the Lyceum of Bologna in 1808, was the cantata in question, which, if not based on the favourite subject of

Orpheus, was at least connected with it. Pianto d'Armonia per la Morte d'Orfeo was at once the subject and the title of this memorable composition. At this period Rossini was an ardent student of Haydn's symphonies and quartets; and after the production of his cantata, which obtained remarkable success, he was appointed director of the Philharmonic concerts, and profited by his position to give a performance of Haydn's Seasons. A distinct reminiscence of this time, and more than a distinct reminiscence of one of the best known melodies in the Seasons, was to be found eight years afterwards in the lively trio ("Zitti, Zitti") of The Barber of Seville.

During his studies at the Lyceum Rossini did not neglect the piano. He entertained a high respect for this admirable instrument, this orchestra on a reduced scale, minus, of course, the variety of timbres; and one of his latest works was a fantasia for pianoforte on airs from L'Africaine, dedicated to his friend Meyerbeer. Rossini used at this time to style himself "pianist of the fourth class;" and that he obtained no higher rank in the pianistic hierarchy is perhaps due to the peculiarity of the instruction he received from his professor at the Lyceum of Bologna, Signor Prinetti. Prinetti taught his pupils to play the scales with the first finger and thumb. A pianist taught to depend on his first finger and thumb to the neglect of the three other fingers could scarcely be expected to graduate very highly in the pianoforte schools.

Rossini was just seventeen years of age when he produced his first symphony, which was followed by a quartet; and a year later he brought out his first opera. During his musical travels in the Romagna, where, among other places, he was in the habit of visiting Lugo, Ferrara, Forli, and Sinigaglia, he had, at the last-named place, inspired with confidence the Marquis Cavalli, director of the local theatre. The marquis was also impresario of the San Mosè Theatre at Venice (the San Mosè, like most other Italian theatres, took its name from the parish to which it belonged), and he wished Rossini to compose an opera for his Venetian establishment. Rossini's previous work had been performed before the professor's pupils and a few invited friends at the Lyceum of Bologna. The opera ordered by the Marquis Cavalli was the first of his works performed before the general public. It was a one-act piece, entitled La Cambiale di Matrimonio. It was given for the first time in 1810 when Rossini was just eighteen years old. The sum paid for it was 200 francs, or, in English money, 8l.

La Cambiale di Matrimonio was succeeded by a cantata on the oft-treated subject of the abandonment of Dido. Didone Abbandonata was composed for a relative, the brilliant Esther Mombelli, and it was performed in 1811. The same year Rossini brought out at Bologna L'Equivoco Stravagante, an opera buffa in two acts. In this work, of which nothing seems to have been preserved, the concerted pieces were much admired. The final rondo, too, is still cited as a type of those final airs for which Rossini seemed to have a particular taste until, after producing the most brilliant specimen of the style in the "Non più mesta" of Cinderella, he left them to the care of other less original composers; for of Rossini's final airs "Non più mesta" was the final one of all.

None of Rossini's earlier operas were engraved; a circumstance which allowed him to borrow from them the best pieces for other works, but which also prevents us in the present day from arriving at any precise idea as to their value and importance.

The first opera of Rossini's which, years afterwards, was deemed worthy the honour of a revival was L'Inganno Felice, composed in 1812 for Venice. It was brought out at Paris in 1819; and the impresario, Barbaja, for whom Rossini composed so many admirable works, gave it at Vienna, where he was carrying on an operatic enterprise simultaneously with two other operatic enterprises at Milan and at Naples.

L'Inganno Felice was the first opera by which Rossini made a decided mark, and such was its success that he was now requested to furnish works for Ferrara, Milan, and Rome. For Ferrara he was to compose an oratorio.

But although Ciro in Babilonia is generally described in the catalogues of Rossini's works as an oratorio, yet, like Mosè in Egitto composed six years later, it was an opera so far as regards form, and was only called an oratorio from the circumstance of its being given in Lent without the usual stage accessories. Ciro in Babilonia was by no means successful as a whole. The composer, however, saved from the wreck of his oratorio two valuable fragments: a chorus which afterwards figured in Aureliano in Palmira, and from which he borrowed the theme of Almaviva's beautiful solo in The Barber of Seville, "Ecco ridente il cielo;" and the concerted finale which, in the year 1827, found its way into the French version of Mosè in Egitto.

Some forty years after the production of Ciro in Babilonia Rossini spoke to Ferdinand Hiller (who has recorded the words in his highly interesting Conversations with Rossini) of a poor woman who had only one good note in her voice, which he accordingly made her repeat while the melody of the solo given to her in Ciro was played by the orchestra. So in the French burlesque of Les Saltimbanques, an untaught player of the trombone is introduced, who, being able to play but one note, is told that that will suffice, and that if he keeps strictly to it "the lovers of that note will be delighted."

CHAPTER II

LA PIETRA DEL PARAGONE

ROSSINI had already written two operas in 1812, and he was destined in this fertile year to produce three more: two at Venice, La Scala di Seta and L'Occasione fa il Ladro; and one at Milan, La Pietra del Paragone.

La Pietra del Paragone was Rossini's next great success after L'Inganno Felice. The leading parts were assigned to Galli, afterwards one of the most famous bass-singers of his time, and to Madame Marcolini, who had played the principal character in L'Equivoco Stravagante, and who had particularly distinguished herself in that work by her singing of the final rondo before mentioned.

In La Pietra del Paragone Madame Marcolini was furnished with a final rondo of the pattern already approved, and in this, as in the earlier one, she gained a most brilliant success.

The libretto of La Pietra del Paragone is founded on an idea at least as old as that of Timon of Athens. Count Asdrubal, surrounded by friends and beloved by a charming young lady, is rash enough to wish to know whether the friendship and the love he seems to have inspired are due to himself and his own personal qualities, or to the riches he is known to possess. To determine the point he causes a bill of exchange for a large sum to be presented at his house. He himself appears in disguise to claim the money; and, in accordance with instructions given beforehand, the count's steward recognises the signature and honours the draft. The sum for which the bill has been made out is so large that to pay it the count's exchequer is absolutely drained. Some few of the friends stand the test well enough, but others, as might have been expected, prove insincere. As for the young lady, the "touchstone" has the effect of bringing out her character in the brightest colours. Timid by nature, she had hitherto refrained from expressing, except in the most reserved manner, the love she really entertains for Count Asdrubal. After his apparent ruin, however, the advances are all from her side; and she finds herself obliged to resort to all kinds of devices in order to compel him to a formal declaration. She even feels called upon to appear—though whether for logical or merely for picturesque reasons can scarcely at this distant date be decided—in a Hussar uniform; and in this striking garb Madame Marcolini sang the celebrated final rondo, saluting the public with her sabre in acknowledgment of their applause, and repeating the salutes again and again as the applause was renewed.

La Pietra del Paragone is quite unknown to the opera-goers of the present day. It belongs to the year 1812, and probably no one now living ever heard it. Many, however, have heard portions of it; for La Pietra del Paragone not having proved thoroughly successful as a whole, the composer extracted the best pieces from it and introduced them into La Cenerentola, which, five years later, was represented for the first time at Rome. The air "Miei rampolli," the duet "Un soave no so chè," the drinking chorus, and the baron's burlesque proclamation, were all borrowed or rather taken once and for ever from the score of La Pietra del Paragone. Some other pieces, too, from the same work were nearly fifty years later heard at least once in an opera attributed to Rossini brought out at Paris in the year 1859. It has been said that among Rossini's operas of the year 1812 were two written for the San Mosè of Venice. The second of these, L'Occasione fa il Ladro, made its appearance substantially at Naples in conjunction with the pieces just spoken of, extracted from La Pietra del Paragone. An Italian poetaster, Signor Berettoni, gave to his new arrangement of L'Occasione fa il Ladro (which, by the way, he had enriched with selections not only from La Pietra del Paragone, but also from Aureliano in Palmira) the title of Un Curioso Accidente.

Rossini, however, though he did not mind borrowing from himself, did not choose to be borrowed from without permission, as without dexterity, by other persons; and finding that a pasticcio made up of pieces taken more or less at random from the works of his youth was to be brought out as a new and original work, he addressed to the manager of the Théâtre des Italiens, M. Calzado, the following letter on the subject:—

"November 11th, 1859..

"SIR,—I am told that the bills of your theatre announce a new opera by me under this title Un Curioso Accidente.

"I do not know whether I have the right to prevent the representation of a production in two acts (more or less) made up of old pieces of mine; I have never occupied myself with questions of this kind in regard to my works (not one of which, by the way, is named Un Curioso Accidente). In any case I have not objected to, and I do not object to, the representation of Un Curioso Accidente. But I cannot allow the public invited to your theatre, and your subscribers to think either that it is a new opera by me or that I took any part in arranging it.

"I must beg of you then to remove from your bills the word new, together with my name as author, and to substitute instead the following:—'Opera, consisting of pieces by M. Rossini, arranged by M. Berettoni.'

"I request that this alteration may appear in the bills of to-morrow, in default of which I shall be obliged to ask from justice what I now ask from your good faith.

"Accept my sincere compliments,

(Signed) "GIOACHINO ROSSINI."

On receiving this letter the manager withdrew the well-named Curioso Accidente, in connection with which no accident was more curious than that of its production. It had already been played once; and at this single representation much success had been obtained by a trio in the buffo style for men's voices borrowed from La Pietra del Paragone, and a duet for soprano and contralto from Aureliano in Palmira.

It is not so easy as it may at first appear to decide which deserves to be considered the first of Rossini's operas. The opera or operetta of La Cambiale di Matrimonio (1810), was the first produced on the stage; and L'Inganno Felice (1812), was the first which made a marked impression, and which, played throughout Italy, at Paris, and at Vienna, gained for its author something like a European reputation. But the first opera that Rossini ever composed was Demetrio e Polibio, which, written in the spring of 1809 when he was just seventeen years old, was produced at Rome—though not until it had undergone a process of retouching—in 1812.

An Italian officer, whom Stendhal met at Como one night when Demetrio e Polibio was to be represented—or perhaps it was the Abbé Carpani who met him; in any case the story is to be found in Stendhal's Life of Rossini—gave this curious account of the Mombelli family, all of whom were connected in one way or another with the performance of Rossini's earliest opera.

"The Mombellis Company," he said, "consists of a single family. Of the two daughters, one, who is always dressed as a man, takes the part of the musico (or sopranist); that is Marianna. The other one, Esther, who has a voice of greater extent though less even, less perfectly sweet, is the prima donna. In Demetrio e Polibio the old Mombelli, who was once a celebrated tenor takes the part of the King. That of the chief of the conspirators will be filled by a person called Olivieri, who has long been attached to Madame Mombelli, the mother, and who, to be useful to the family, takes utility parts on the stage and acts in the house as cook and major domo. Without being pretty, the Mombellis have pleasing faces. But they are ferociously virtuous, and it is supposed that the father, who is an ambitious man, wishes to get them married."

Madame Mombelli, moreover, had written the libretto, while the old Mombelli—once a "celebrated tenor" and still "so ambitious" as to wish to see his daughters legitimately married—had from among his plentiful reminiscences given Rossini ideas for melodies. Not only did the company, in the words of Stendhal's officer, consist of a single family; this family included, moreover, among its members, the composer himself, who was somehow related to the Mombellis.

From 1812 to 1813 was for Rossini a great step in advance; for during this latter year were produced Tancredi and L'Italiana in Algeri, works destined within a very short time to find their way all over Europe. But before producing Tancredi, Rossini began the year by bringing out a little operetta entitled Il Figlio per Azzardo.

Rossini caused in his time a great deal of trouble to managers; and if those with whom he had to deal were for the most part bald, that, he said, was to be accounted for by his having driven them repeatedly to tear their hair. Some of the directors suffered from his apparent laziness, which at most could be called dilatoriness; for that Rossini was a composer of extraordinary activity is shown by the fact that by the time he was thirty-seven he had written thirty-seven operas; while, during the period of his greatest fertility, he frequently produced as many as four operas in one year. More than once, too, he completed an opera within a fortnight; but this fortnight was usually the last and never the first of the space of time assigned to him for the composition of a given work. Sometimes, however, he was annoyed and worried by managers without sufficient cause; and in these cases he knew how to retaliate. The manager of the San Mosè theatre, that Marquis Cavalli who also directed the theatre of Sinigaglia, and who, as already mentioned, had given Rossini his first commission, thought that having begun by writing for the San Mosè, the young composer ought not to work for any other theatre at Venice. He had engaged, however, to write an opera for the Fenice, where Tancredi was destined to be brought out; and the Marquis was so annoyed at this that he treated Rossini on more than one occasion with absolute incivility. He had supplied him, moreover, with a libretto so monstrously absurd that it was impossible to treat it seriously, or even in the spirit of mere comedy. Rossini, however, had to choose between setting this nonsense to music or paying a fine; and he preferred the former alternative. The task he now set himself was to compose to his ridiculous libretto music more ridiculous even than the words. Tenor music was given to the bass, who, to execute it, had to shout at the top of his voice. The soprano, on the other hand, had been furnished with a contralto part, which made demands only upon the lowest notes of her voice. A singer of notorious-incompetence was provided with a most difficult air, accompanied pianissimo, so that his faults might at least not be concealed. Another singer, whose burlesque appearance never failed to throw the house into convulsions, had to sing a sentimental melody of the most lackadaisical kind. The orchestration was quite as remarkable as the writing for the voices. One of Rossini's great merits consists in his having introduced new instruments into the operatic orchestra of his time; and in scoring Il Figlio per Azzardo, he wrote parts for instruments of percussion never before and probably never afterwards employed. These were the tin-shades of the candles with which the desks of the players were furnished, and which, in one movement, had to be struck at the beginning of each bar. For a time the public smiled at Rossini's pleasantry, until at last it occurred to some one that the composer was taking liberties with his audience. Then hoots and hisses were heard from every part of the theatre, and the end of Rossini's practical joke was that the practical joker had to rush from his post at the head of the orchestra and seek safety in flight.

CHAPTER III

ITALIAN OPERA UNTIL THE TIME OF ROSSINI

Tancredi was Rossini's first serious opera, and the first opera by which his name became known throughout Europe. In this work, too, we find indicated, if not fully carried out, all those changes in the composition of the lyric drama which, without absolutely inventing them, he introduced from Germany, and especially from Mozart's operas, into Italy.

It seems strange, what was nevertheless the case, that when Rossini began to write, the mere forms of the lyric drama were, in Italy at least, far from being looked upon as settled. Opera could not at that time boast a history of more than about two centuries, and though it had made great progress during the previous hundred years and was scarcely the same entertainment as that which the most illustrious nobles in Italy had taken under their protection in the early part of the seventeenth century, it was still far from resembling the opera of the present day; so much more developed, so much more elaborated.

No general view of the progress of operatic art in Europe can well be taken; for its advance has been different in each country. But its progress in Italy was sufficiently regular from its birth, or rather its invention, towards the end of the sixteenth century up to the period of Scarlatti; and from Scarlatti in a continuous line to Rossini.

Without going back to the origin of music in general, it may not be inappropriate, in connection with Rossini's innovations, and with a view to these innovations being better understood, to sketch in the briefest manner the history of the musical drama in Italy from its deliberate invention until, after its various developments, it became what Rossini made it between the years 1813, the year in which Tancredi was brought out, and 1823, the date of the production of Semiramide.

The opera, so far as a natural origin can be claimed for it at all, proceeds from the sacred musical plays of the fifteenth and sixteenth centuries, as the modern drama proceeds from the so-called mysteries of the same period. Indeed the earliest musical dramas of modern Italy, from which the opera of the present day is directly descended, were mysteries differing only from the dramatic mysteries in having been written for the singing, not for the speaking voice. The opera, or drama in music, is not, compared with the spoken drama, a very ancient form of art. Persons afflicted with a rage for seeking in the distant past traces and origins of a form of art which was created and forced into existence in comparatively modern times, see the first specimens of opera in the Greek plays; a view which will be worth considering when writers on the subject of Greek music have come to an understanding as to its exact nature. One thing is quite certain, that the Greek plays are remembered solely by what musicians call the "words," whereas, with the exception of Herr Wagner's highly poetical, highly dramatic works, there are no operas written to be performed throughout in music, which, by their words alone, would have the least chance of living. Nor did the musical mysteries or musical plays of the fifteenth century—which were partly declaimed, partly sung, and always by solo voices—bear any great resemblance to the grand operas of the present day with their airs, duets, concerted pieces, and elaborate dramatic finales, supported by an orchestra which is always being varied and reinforced through the addition of new instruments, and in which composers aim constantly at the formation of new instrumental combinations. Of course, too, the sacred musical plays of the fifteenth century differed from our modern operas by their subjects. A primitive sort of opera on the Conversion of St. Paul, which was performed throughout in music at Rome in 1440, is not the sort of work that would be likely to interest our modern audiences, who entertain a marked preference for operas in which a leading part is assigned to the prima donna, and who have no objection to the prima donna's representing a thoroughly mundane character, such as the fascinating Carmen, in the late M. Bizet's opera of that name, or the less fascinating Violetta, in Verdi's Traviata.

The first opera on a profane, or rather on a secular subject—for it is surely a mistake to regard everything not sacred as necessarily profane—was the descent of Orpheus into the infernal regions, drawn thither, as is well known, by his wife, Eurydice. The subject of Orpheus, alike lyrical and dramatic, has been a favourite one with composers for the last four hundred years, from Poliziano, who produced his Orfeo at Rome in 1440, up to Gluck, nearly three centuries later, and from Gluck down to Offenbach, who delights a good many persons in the present day. The Orfeo, which was brought out just four centuries ago, at Rome, bore no more resemblance, in a musical point of view, to a modern opera, than did the sacred musical plays before spoken of; and up to the year 1600 we meet with no musical work which bears more than a fundamental or general sort of resemblance to the modern opera. But almost immediately after the production of the second Eurydice a great reformer appeared. Monteverde, the innovator in question, changed, or at least gave new development to, the harmonic system of his predecessors, assigned far greater importance in his operas to accompaniments, and increased greatly both the number and the variety of the instruments in the orchestra, which, under his arrangement, included every kind of instrument known at the time. Monteverde employed a separate combination of instruments to announce the entry and return of each personage in his operas; a dramatic means made use of long afterwards by Hoffmann—better known by his fantastic tales than by his musical works—in his opera of Undine; and which cannot but suggest a similar device employed with more system and with greater elaboration by Wagner.

Monteverde, like so many of his predecessors and followers, felt attracted by the story of Orpheus and Eurydice, and his first work was on the subject of Orfeo, which was produced in 1608 at the Court of Mantua; ordered, it may be, by that gallant but dissolute Duke of Mantua whom Signor Mario used to impersonate so admirably in Rigoletto. Monteverde's Orfeo contained parts for harpsichords, lyres, violas, double basses, a double harp with two rows of strings, two violins, besides guitars, organs, a flute, clarions, and even trombones. It is interesting to know that, apart from the instrumental combinations which announced the entry and return of each character, the bass-violas accompanied Orpheus; the violas, Eurydice; the trombones, Pluto; the organs, Apollo; while Charon—a most unsentimental personage, one would think— sang to the accompaniment of that sentimental instrument, the guitar.

I have, of course, no intention of following out the history of opera from Monteverde to Verdi. It will be sufficient to remark that Monteverde, the real founder of opera in something like its present form, produced a number of works at Venice, until at last the fame of the Venetian operas spread throughout Italy, so that by the middle of the seventeenth century the new entertainment was established at Verona, Bologna, Rome, Turin, Naples, and Messina. Opera, whatever its merits and defects, is essentially a royal and aristocratic entertainment. The drama was started by Thespis in a cart. The opera, on the other hand, was founded by popes, cardinals, and kings. The first operatic libretto, that of Poliziano's Orfeo, was the work of Cardinal Riario, nephew of Sixtus IV. Pope Clement IX. was the author of no less than seven libretti. The popes, indeed, used, in former days, to keep up an excellent theatre; and even in these degenerate times the taste for music has not, or had not until lately, died out at the Vatican.

It has been said that the history of opera, though Italy cannot claim to have been the one scene of its development, can be more conveniently because more continuously traced in Italy than in the various European countries where it has been cultivated, and where, in the case of three of these countries—Italy, Germany, and France,—it has made distinct advances. Nor, in considering the history of opera in Italy, is it necessary to observe its progress in Italy generally. It is sufficient to note the changes through which it passed at Naples alone. From Scarlatti (end of the seventeenth to the middle of the eighteenth century) to the immediate predecessors of Rossini, the history of the development of the opera in Italy is indeed the history of its development at Naples; and though, unlike previous celebrated composers, Rossini did not pursue his studies at Naples, he soon made Naples his head-quarters, and produced at the San Carlo theatre between the years 1815 and 1823 all his best Italian operas in the serious style: Otello, for instance, La Donna del Lago and Semiramide.

Scarlatti, the founder of the great Neapolitan school, studied at Rome under Carrissimi; and he is memorable in musical history as having given new development to the operatic air, while he introduced for the first time measured recitative. Of Scarlatti's immediate followers, Logroscino and Durante, the former introduced concerted pieces and the dramatic finale which afterwards received new development at the hands of Piccinni. This important feature to which modern opera owes so much of its importance and so much of its effect, was introduced into serious opera by Paisiello. Paisiello, like Scarlatti, Logroscino and Durante, was professor at the Conservatorio of Naples; and under his guidance were formed Jomelli, Piccinni, Sacchini, Guglielmi, and Cimarosa. The particular innovations due to Piccinni and Paisiello have already been mentioned. Cimarosa composed the best overtures which, up to his time, the Italian school could boast of, and he was the first to introduce quartets and other concerted pieces in the midst of dramatic action; not, that is to say, as ornaments at the end of an act, which hitherto had been the place conventionally assigned to them, but as integral parts of the musical drama. This innovation occurs for the first time in Il Fanatico per gli antichi Romani, which Cimarosa composed in 1773. It was not until nineteen years afterwards that this master produced his Matrimonio Segreto. But meanwhile Cimarosa had been completely distanced by Mozart, who, himself a great inventor, and, so to say, anticipator, adopted moreover everything that was worth adopting in the methods of all his contemporaries and predecessors.

To resume, in as few words as possible, the history of opera in Italy up to the time of Rossini, this form of art was at first nothing but recitative, or recitative with a chorus at the end of each act. Then occasional airs were introduced, then duets; and it is not until the middle of the eighteenth century that we find an example of an operatic trio. Quartets and dramatic finales followed in due course; and while the Italians had been developing new methods of employing the solo voices, Gluck had given prominence to the chorus as a dramatic factor, and had cultivated choral writing with the happiest effect. Other Germans, with Haydn foremost among them, had produced new orchestral combinations, until at last Mozart joined to the vocal forms of the Italians the instrumental forms of the Germans, while developing and perfecting both. Rossini introduced quite gradually into Italian opera those reforms which are particularly associated with his name; and perhaps in no other way could he have got them accepted. But he might, had he felt so disposed, have borrowed them one and all in a piece from the works of Mozart.

Let it be remembered, however, as a matter of fact, that when in 1813 Rossini produced Tancredi, which marks the commencement of the reforms introduced by him into serious opera, he had enjoyed no opportunity of seeing any of Mozart's works on the stage. Probably he had studied the music of Mozart, as we know him to have studied that of Haydn, in score; but it was not until 1814 that Don Giovanni, nor until 1815 that the Marriage of Figaro, was performed for the first time in Italy at the Scala theatre.

Rossini's success, due above all to the fascinating character of his easily appreciable melodies, was instantaneous; and it spread like wild-fire from Italy all over Europe. More than a quarter of a century, however, passed before Mozart's great works made their way from Vienna to the chief cities of Italy, and to the capitals of France and England. This tardy recognition of Mozart's dramatic genius may be explained in part by the outbreak of the French revolution soon after their production, and by the wars which distracted Europe from the time of the French revolution until the pacification of 1815.

CHAPTER IV

TANCREDI

Tancredi, composed a year after La Pietra del Paragone, was Rossini's first serious opera. It was also the first opera by which he became known throughout Europe.

To amateurs of the present day its melodies appear of old-fashioned, or at least of antique cast. The recitatives seem long, and they are interminable compared with those by which Verdi connects his musical pieces. But when Tancredi was first brought out opera seria consisted almost entirely of recitative, relieved here and there and only at long intervals by solo airs. For much of this declamation Rossini substituted singing; for endless monologues and dialogues supported by a few chords, concerted pieces connected and supported by a brilliant orchestral accompaniment.

Rossini, in fact, introduced into serious opera the forms which comic opera already possessed. The parts were at that time differently distributed in opera seria and opera buffa; and in the latter less restricted style the bass singer was not as a matter of course kept in the background. Tancredi was the first serious opera in which a certain prominence was given to the bass, though it was not until some years later—in Otello, 1816, in La Gazza Ladra, 1817, and in Mosè, 1818—that Rossini ventured to entrust bass singers with leading parts. Opera seria, when

Rossini was beginning his career, was governed by rules as strict, as formal, and as thoroughly conventional as those which gave so much artificiality and so much dulness to the classical drama of France. The company for comic opera consisted of the primo buffo (tenor), prima buffa, buffo caricato (bass), seconda buffa, and ultima parte (bass). The company for serious opera was made up of the primo uomo (soprano), prima donna, and tenor, the secondo uomo (soprano), seconda donna, and ultima parte (bass); and in serious opera the ultima parte was not only kept in the background, but, except in concerted pieces, was scarcely ever heard.

As a solo singer, the bass in serious opera had no existence. Gradually Rossini brought him forward, until he became at last as prominent as the tenor, or even more so. In Semiramide, for instance, the principal male character is Assur. In Tancredi, from which Semiramide is separated by an interval of ten years, the bass has little to do. He already, however, possesses an importance which was denied to him in the serious operas of Rossini's predecessors.

In Tancredi, again, the composer introduces concerted pieces in situations where, had the ancient method been followed, there would have been only monologues. In these concerted pieces, moreover, the dramatic action is kept up, whereas the endless monologues and long sequences of airs which gave such character as they possessed to the operas of Rossini's immediate predecessors had the effect of delaying it. To musical reformers of a later period Rossini himself seemed to insert songs in his operas merely for the sake of singing, and greatly to the injury of the drama. But he diminished considerably the number of formal airs which, until he began to write, were included as a matter of course in every opera. He increased the number of characters, and made, for the first time in Italian opera, a free use of the chorus, which in the works of the old school plays quite a subordinate part and has no dramatic functions assigned to it at all.

Rossini's innovations are well described by Lord Mount-Edgcumbe, who has no praise, however, to bestow upon them, but on the contrary, condemns them without measure. Indeed, the more he blames Rossini, the more he calls attention to what are now recognised as his chief merits. When Lord Mount-Edgcumbe undertakes to show how Rossini was ruining the musical drama, he in fact points out how he was reforming it. "So great a change," he writes, "has taken place in the character of the (operatic) dramas, in the style of the music and its performance, that I cannot help enlarging upon that subject before we proceed further. One of the most material alterations is that the grand distinction between serious and comic operas is nearly at an end, the separation of the singers for their performances entirely so. Not only do the same sing in both, but a new species of drama has arisen, a kind of mongrel between them, called semi-seria, which bears the same analogy to the other two that the nondescript melodrama does to the legitimate tragedy and comedy of the English stage. The construction of these newly invented pieces," continues Lord Mount-Edgcumbe, "is essentially different from the old. The dialogue, which used to be carried on in recitative, and which in Metastasio's operas is often so beautiful and interesting, is now cut up (and rendered unintelligible if it were worth listening to) into pezzi concertati, or long singing conversations, which present a tedious succession of unconnected, ever-changing motivos, having nothing to do with each other; and if a satisfactory air is for a moment introduced, which the ear would like to dwell upon, to hear modulated, varied, and again returned to, it is broken off, before it is well understood, by a sudden transition into a totally different melody, time, and key, and recurs no more, so that no impression can be made or recollection of it preserved. Single songs are almost exploded ... even the prima donna, who would formerly have complained at having less than three or four airs allotted to her, is now satisfied with one trifling cavatina for a whole opera."

In his valuable attack upon Rossini, Lord Mount-Edgcumbe is admirably sincere. After condemning Rossini for his new distribution of characters, and for his employment of bass voices in leading parts, "to the manifest injury of melody and total subversion of harmony, in which the lowest part is their peculiar province," he calls attention to the fact that Mozart has previously sinned in like manner; and he cannot help expressing some astonishment when he reflects "that the principal characters in two of Mozart's operas have been written for basses." It might have occurred to him, moreover, that Mozart, both in Don Giovanni and in the Magic Flute, united the serious with the comic, and, indeed, that there was not one of the so-called innovations charged against Rossini, which were not in reality due to Mozart. In Italy, where Mozart's works were at the time unknown, Rossini may well have appeared a perfectly original genius, not only by his richness of melodic invention, but also by the novelty of his forms. But it is strange that an amateur, acquainted, as Lord Mount-Edgcumbe was, with the works of Mozart, should not at once have perceived that Rossini, in introducing so much which was new only to the Italians, was making no bold experiment, but was merely following in the wake of a greater inventor than himself.

The success, however, of Rossini's first serious opera was due less to new methods of distributing parts and of constructing pieces than to the beauty of the melodies. Stendhal, in his always ingenious but seldom quite veracious Vie de Rossini, dwells on the sort of fever with which its tuneful themes inspired the whole Venetian population, so that even in the law-courts the judges, he relates, were obliged to direct the ushers to stop the singing of "Di tanti palpiti" and "Mi rivedrai ti rivedrò." "I thought that after hearing my opera," wrote Rossini himself, "the Venetians would think me mad. Not at all: I found they were much madder than I was."

"It is said at Venice," writes Stendhal, "that the first idea of this delicious cantilena, which expresses so well the joy of meeting after a long absence, is taken from a Greek litany; Rossini had heard it a few days before at vespers in the church of one of the little islands of the lagoons of Venice."

"Since its production," says M. Azevedo, "on the stage and in the universe, it has been made the subject of a canticle for the Catholic Church, like all other successful airs. But a litany before the air, and a canticle after the air, are not the same thing."

In connection with Tancredi, mention has been made of Rossini's reforms in serious opera, which he found too serious. Comic opera, on the other hand, as it existed up to his time, seemed to him too comic or rather, too extravagant. We have seen that the old opera buffa had its separate set of characters and singers, and its own separate style, musical as well as dramatic. Rossini raised the level of the style, and for farce substituted comedy. In the midst, too, of comedy airs, he introduced, from time to time, a sentimental one such as "Ecco ridente" in Il Barbiere, and "Languir per una bella," in L'Italiana in Algeri—which Rossini brought out at Milan (1813) soon after the production of Tancredi at Venice, and which holds among his comic operas the same position that belongs to Tancredi among his serious ones.

Italian audiences had been trained to disapprove of the same singer appearing one night in a comic and the next in a tragic part; and critical hearers are said to have been shocked at seeing the same artist appear successively as Figaro and as Assur, as Dr. Bartolo and as Mosè. Apart from the substitution of the comic for the farcical in the general treatment, L'Italiana in Algeri is remarkable as the first comic opera in which Rossini introduced that crescendo, which was soon recognised as a characteristic feature in all his works. He had already tested its effect in the overture to Tancredi—the first Italian overture which became popular apart from the work to which it belonged—and in the concerted finale of the same opera. Rossini is said to have borrowed this effect from Paisiello's Re Teodoro. But the invention of the crescendo was energetically claimed by Mosca, who had certainly employed it before Rossini, and who regarded it as his own private property; circulating, in order to establish his prior right, copies of a piece composed long before Tancredi was brought out, in which fully developed crescendi occurred. This did not prevent Rossini from continuing to write crescendi, nor from being satirised and caricatured as "Signor Crescendo," when, some ten years afterwards, he went to Paris.

CHAPTER V

OPERATIC CUSTOMS IN ROSSINI'S TIME

THE year after the production of Tancredi, Rossini, in 1814, brought out Aureliano, which was not successful. It contained, however, at least one piece of music which the composer, with due regard to economy, was determined not to waste. This was the introduction itself, borrowed from Ciro in Babilonia, which, when Rossini afterwards adapted its melody to words written for Count Almaviva in the Barber of Seville, obtained lasting success in the form of the charming cavatina "Ecco ridente il cielo."

The overture, moreover, to Aureliano in Palmira, after serving as instrumental introduction to Elisabetta, produced a year later at Naples, found ultimately a permanent position as musical preface to the Barber of Seville. The failure of Aureliano in Palmira, which Rossini attributed in a great measure to the liberties taken with the music by at least one of the performers, caused him to adopt the practice of writing for the singers the very notes he intended them to sing. Strange innovation! But, until Rossini's time, the vocalists were really the composer's masters, and regarded his airs merely as so much canvas for embroidery.

To Rossini belongs the honour of having helped greatly to expel the sopranists from the operatic stage. The Church, with a view to soprano voices in choirs, from which women were excluded, had introduced them; and ultimately the Church pronounced against them. But nothing could have had a greater effect in putting them down than Rossini's absolute refusal to write for them, or to allow them to sing in those of his operas performed under his direct superintendence.

The circumstances under which Rossini broke with the most celebrated sopranist of his time—that Velluti, whom a wit described as "non vir sed veluti"—are worth relating. Rossini had written for this personage a part in his Aureliano in Palmira (1814), the most celebrated of his very few failures; and the composer soon found that the singer had no respect for his music, which he treated as so much substance for elaboration and pretended adornment; while the singer discovered that the composer was so narrow-minded as to require his melodies to be sung as he had thought fit to write them. In those days dramatic propriety and music itself were sacrificed to the vocalists, who, far from studying parts, do not seem, in any true spirit, to have mastered airs. We read of singers having been kept to scales and passages for years at a time; and every one who takes an interest in musical history must remember the burlesque exclamation of Porpora, who, when Caffarelli had practised nothing but exercises with him for no less than five years, cried out: "You have nothing more to learn! Caffarelli is the first singer in the world!"

Aureliano was not played after the first night: and Rossini had the satisfaction of hearing that though his opera had failed, Velluti had made a brilliant success in the principal part. Velluti had, in fact, astonished and delighted the public by his vocal gymnastics. But it was not Rossini's music, it was really his own music, suggested by Rossini's, that he had sung.

Unable—perhaps even unwilling—to run altogether counter to the prevailing taste, Rossini continued to write highly florid music. But he supplied his own decorations, and made them so elaborate that the most skilful adorner would have found it difficult to add to them.

Writing for a French public Rossini showed, in William Tell, that he was as much a master of the simple dramatic style in which the singer has not to display vocal agility, but to express human emotion, as he was already known to be of the highly decorative style admired by the Italians. "Rossini," says Stendhal, in his interesting account of the first representation of Aureliano in Palmira, which he claims to have witnessed, "followed in his first works the style of his predecessors. He respected the voices, and only thought of bringing about the triumph of singing. Such is the system in which he composed Demetrio e Polibio, L'Inganno felice, La Pietra del Paragone, Tancredi, &c. Rossini had found La Marcolini, La Malanotte, La Manfredini, the Mombelli family, why should he not endeavour to give prominence to the singing—he who is such a good singer, and who when he sits down to the piano to sing one of his own airs, seems to transform the genius we know him to possess as a composer into that of a singer? The fact is, a little event took place which at once changed the composer's views.... Rossini arrived at Milan in 1814, to write Aureliano in Palmira. There he met with Velluti, who was to sing in his opera; Velluti, then in the flower of his youth and talent, one of the best-looking men of his time, and much given to abuse his prodigious resources. Rossini had never

36

heard this singer. He wrote a cavatina for him. At the first rehearsal, with full orchestra, he heard Velluti sing it, and was struck with admiration. At the second rehearsal Velluti began to embroider (fiorire). Rossini found some of his effects admirable, and still approved; but at the third rehearsal, the richness of the embroidery was such that it quite concealed the body of the air. At last the grand day of the first representation arrived. The cavatina, and all Velluti's part, was enthusiastically applauded; but Rossini could scarcely recognise what Velluti was singing; he did not know his own music. However, Velluti's singing was very beautiful and wonderfully successful with the public, which, after all, does no wrong in applauding what gives it so much pleasure. The pride of the young composer was deeply wounded; the opera failed, and the sopranist alone succeeded. Rossini's lively perception saw at once all that such an event could suggest. 'It is by a fortunate accident,' he said to himself, 'that Velluti happens to be a singer of taste, but how am I to know that at the next theatre I write for I shall not find another singer, who, with a flexible throat and an equal mania for fioriture, will not spoil my music so as to render it not only unrecognisable to me, but also wearisome to the public, or at least remarkable only for some details of execution? The danger to my unfortunate music is the more imminent, insomuch as there are no more singing schools in Italy. The theatres are full of artists who have picked up music from singing-masters about the country. This style of singing violin concertos, endless variations, will not only destroy all talent for singing, but will also vitiate the public taste. All the singers will be imitating Velluti, each according to his means. We shall have no more cantilenas; they would be thought poor and cold. Everything will undergo a change, even to the nature of the voices, which, once accustomed to embroider and overlay a cantilena with elaborate ornaments, will soon lose the habit of singing sustained legato passages, and be unable to execute them. I must change my system then. I know how to sing; every one acknowledges that I possess that talent; my fioriture will be in good taste; moreover, I shall discover at once the strong and weak points of my singers, and shall only write for them what they will be able to execute. I will not leave them a place for adding the least apoggiatura. The fioriture, the ornaments, must form an integral part of the air, and be all written in the score.'"

The sopranists might, at an earlier period, have been sent with advantage to Berlin, where, as Dr. Burney tells us, Frederick the Great, taking up his position in the pit of his opera-house immediately behind the conductor of the orchestra, on whose score he kept his eye, would never allow a singer to alter a single passage in his part. The conductor's authority does not seem to have been sufficient, for, according to Burney, it was the king who, when the vocalist took liberties with the score, called upon him to keep to the notes as written by the composer. "The sopranists," says M. Castil-Blaze,[2] "were at all times extremely insolent. They forced the greatest masters to conform to their caprices. They changed, transformed everything to suit their own vanity. They would insist on having an air or a duet placed in such a scene, written in such a style, with such an accompaniment. They were the kings, the tyrants of theatres, managers, and composers; that is why, in the most serious works of the greatest masters of the last century, there occur long cold

---

[2] Théâtres Lyriques de Paris, "L'Opéra, Italien," p. 317.

passages of vocalisation which had been exacted by the sopranists for the sake of exhibiting, in a striking manner, the agility and power of their throats. 'You will be kind enough to sing my music and not yours,' said the venerable and formidable Guglielmi, to a certain virtuoso, threatening him at the same time with his sword. In fact the vocal music, and the whole Italian lyrical system of the eighteenth century, was much more the work of the singers than of the composers."

After the production of Aureliano in Palmira, Rossini for about eighteen months was comparatively idle; for during this period he only produced two operas, Il Turco in Italia, and Sigismondo, of which the former has long ceased to-be played, while the latter was never at any time much performed. Il Turco in Italia was a pendant to L'Italiana in Algeri, but it obtained no greater amount of public favour than continuations usually meet with. The hero of the work was supposed to have been wrecked on the Italian coast, and a like fate awaited the work itself. Rossini, according to his custom, saved what he could from the wreck, and the overture to the Turk in Italy was, some years later, when Otello was brought out, made to do duty as introduction to the story of the Moor of Venice.

As for Sigismondo, the story of its failure was graphically recorded by Rossini himself; who, writing to his mother the same night, enclosed her the outline of a small bottle or fiasco.

Rossini's increasing fame had, among other effects, that of making him visit all the principal cities in Italy. As in his youth he had moved about in his character of conductor from one little town in the Romagna to another, so now, when he had attained his full powers, he was called upon to travel from Bologna to Venice, from Venice to Milan, from Milan to Naples, from Naples to Rome. The two leading theatres of the Peninsula were then, as now, the San Carlo of Naples, and the Scala of Milan. The former received a subvention of 12,000l. from the King of Naples, the latter one of 8,000l. from the Emperor of Austria. These opera-houses, at that time the first in the world, received additional support from public gambling saloons adjoining them; and it was as a waiter at one of these auxiliary establishments that Barbaja, the most illustrious impresario of his own or of any other time—Barbaja, who is mentioned in one of Balzac's novels, and introduced by Scribe in his libretto of La Sirène—commenced his career. Besides the cities already named, Turin, Florence, Bergamo, Genoa, Leghorn, Sienna, Ferrara, had all their opera-houses; some of which were supported by state grants, others by grants from the municipality. Occasionally, too, the necessary operatic subvention was furnished by some local magnate, who either made a liberal donation or constituted himself director of the theatre. The chief towns maintained several opera-houses. There were three at Venice—the Fenice, the San Benedetto, and the San Mosè; and five at Rome—the Argentina, the Valle, the Apollo, the Alberto, and the Tordinona. Next to San Carlo and La Scala ranked the Fenice, and next to the Fenice the Court Theatre of Turin where, inasmuch as it formed part of the king's palace, it was considered 'disrespectful to appear in a cloak, disrespectful to laugh, and disrespectful to applaud till the queen had applauded.'

From 1815 to 1823 Rossini wrote principally for Naples. But we have seen that he also worked for Bologna, Venice, and Milan;

and he composed for the opera-houses of Rome, Il Barbiere, brought out at the Argentina Theatre, La Cenerentola, produced at the Valle Theatre, and Matilda di Sabran, performed for the first time at the Apollo Theatre. At the Fenice of Venice, Rossini's first opera in the serious style, Tancredi (1813), and also his last in that style, Semiramide (1823), were produced. For the Court Theatre of Turin Rossini wrote nothing.

Each of the great Italian opera-houses made a point of bringing out at least two new operas every year; and as the minor theatres were also frequently supplied with new works there was no lack of opportunity for composers anxious to place themselves before the public. The composers were not liberally paid by managers—40l. was considered a fair price for an opera; while from the publishers they received absolutely nothing for the right of engraving. It has already been mentioned that Rossini never troubled himself about the publication of his works, and that he profited by the fact of their not having been engraved to borrow from his failures pieces which, had the scores been before the public, he must have hesitated to re-adopt.

The operas of that day were in two acts; a division which, when the subject was an important one, scarcely conduced to the maintenance of dramatic interest. It was the custom of the time, however, to separate these two acts by a ballet; and thus kept apart they were not found so long, so interminable, as, performed one after the other without a break, our modern audiences would find them.

CHAPTER VI
ROSSINI AT NAPLES

BARBAJA, the ex-waiter at the Ridotto of the San Carlo Theatre, was director of the San Carlo itself, and almost at the height of his glory, which Rossini was so much to increase, when Tancredi was brought out at Venice and L'Italiana in Algeri at Milan.

The year following was not for Rossini a very brilliant one; and neither Aureliano in Palmira, nor a cantata called Egle e Irene, written for the Princess Belgiojoso, nor Il Turco in Italia—all of the year 1814—did much to increase his reputation. But the success of Tancredi and of L'Italiana in Algeri was enough for Barbaja, who accordingly invited Rossini in 1814 to come to Naples and compose something for the San Carlo. On his arrival Rossini signed a contract with Barbaja for several years; binding himself to write two new operas annually, and to re-arrange the music of any old works the manager might wish to produce, either at his principal theatre or at the second Neapolitan opera-house, the Teatro del Fondo, of which also Barbaja was lessee. Rossini's emoluments were to be 40l. (200 ducats) a month with a share in the profits of the gambling saloon. Such an engagement would not seem very magnificent to a second or third rate composer of our own time. But it was better than 40l. an opera, at which rate Rossini had hitherto been paid. Provided, moreover, that he supplied Barbaja with his two new operas every year he was at liberty to write for other managers.

In the present day it is not uncommon to find an operatic manager of enterprise directing two lyrical theatres in two different countries. Mr. Lumley was manager at the same time of Her Majesty's Theatre in London and of the Théâtre des Italiens in Paris. The late Mr. Gye entered into an arrangement (which however was not carried out) for directing the Imperial Opera House of St. Petersburg, while he was at the same time managing the Royal Italian Opera of London. Mr. Mapleson directs simultaneously Her Majesty's Theatre in London, and the Italian Opera which he has recently established at the so-called Academy of Music in New York. But these feats are nothing compared with the performances of Barbaja in the managerial line. It is much easier at the present time to get from London to New York or from London to St. Petersburg, than it was in the days of Barbaja to move from Naples or even from Milan to Vienna; and a manager must have possessed great administrative ability who could direct three operatic enterprises in three different capitals at the same time.

Barbaja had in his employment all the great composers and all the best singers of his native Italy. So numerous was his company that he scarcely knew who did and who did not belong to it; and a story is told of his meeting one day a singer of some celebrity, and offering him an engagement—when, to his consternation and horror, the vocalist informed him that he had been drawing a regular salary from the theatre for the last three months. "Go to Donizetti," cried Barbaja, "and tell him to give you a part without a moment's delay."

On one occasion Donizetti, engaged at that time as accompanist at the Scala Theatre, had been requested to try the voice of a lady who had come to Barbaja with a letter of recommendation. Donizetti asked her to go through a few exercises in solfeggio; on which Barbaja, mistaking do, re, mi, &c., for the words of some outlandish tongue, exclaimed that it would be useless to sing in a foreign language, and that the postulant for an engagement had better carry her talents elsewhere. Another time, when a favourite vocalist complained that the piano, to whose accompaniment she had been rehearsing her part, was too high, Barbaja at once promised that before the next rehearsal he would have it lowered. The following morning the instrument was, as before, half a note above the requisite pitch. It was pointed out to Barbaja that the piano still wanted lowering; upon which he flew into a violent passion and, summoning one of the stage carpenters, asked him why, when he had been told that the piano was too high, he had not shortened it by two or three inches instead of doing so only by one.

When his singers were genuinely successful he would take their part under all circumstances, and defend them against every attack. A popular prima donna told him one day, on arriving at the San Carlo Theatre, whither she had been borne in a sedan-chair, that one of the carriers had been very negligent in his duty, and had allowed her several times to be bumped on the ground. Barbaja called the porters to his room and, giving each a box on the ears, exclaimed, "Which of you two brutes was in fault?"

For the sake of teasing Barbaja, a few of the subscribers to the Scala Theatre agreed one night to hiss Rubini in one of his best parts. Barbaja, perfectly aghast, looked from his box, shook his fist at the seeming malcontents, and, alike indignant and enthusiastic, called out to the universally-admired tenor: "Bravo, Rubini, never mind those pigs! It is I who pay you, and I am delighted with your singing."

In spite of his long-continued success, Barbaja ended, like so many managers, by failing; and but that he stood well with the Austrian Government, who gave him a contract for building barracks at Milan, he might have died in poverty. There is nothing, however, to show that his collapse was due to ignorance of music. It would be probably nearer the truth to attribute it to that loss of energy and tact by which advancing years are generally accompanied.

Among the prime donne of the San Carlo Theatre Barbaja's favourite, in the fullest sense of the word, was Mademoiselle Colbran, who, after studying under Crescentini and Marinelli, made her first appearance with brilliant success at Paris in 1801. She was then but sixteen years of age, having been born at Madrid in 1785. When Rossini, then, first met her at Naples in 1815, she was already thirty. Her voice began to deteriorate soon afterwards, if we are to believe Stendhal—who, much as he had in common with the Abbé Carpani (including nearly the whole of the materials for his Life of Rossini), did not share that writer's admiration for a singer whom it was the fashion for royalists to laud, for republicans to decry. Stendhal, though he feared that opera, accustomed to subventions and to patronage of all kinds, could not flourish under republican institutions, was nevertheless inclined towards republicanism.

Mademoiselle Colbran has been described as a great beauty in the queenly style—dark hair, brilliant eyes, imposing demeanour; and though Stendhal is under the impression that her voice began to fall off soon after Rossini's arrival at Naples, it seems certain that she must have preserved it in all its beauty until long afterwards. Rossini in any case wrote for her many of his best parts which, had they not been perfectly sung, could scarcely have met with the success they actually obtained. Among these parts may be mentioned in particular those of Desdemona, Elcia in Mosè in Egitto, Elena in La Donna del Lago, Zelmira in the opera of that name, and Semiramide. The artistic merits of Mademoiselle Colbran were, however, as has already been mentioned, discussed habitually from a political point of view. Revolutionists hissed her because the king admired her, while royalists were ready under all circumstances to applaud her. The first part which Rossini composed for Mademoiselle Colbran, his future wife, was that of Elisabetta in the opera of the same name; a work founded on Scott's novel of Kenilworth, and written appropriately enough by a certain Signor Smith. Smith's knowledge of the English language seems, in spite of his name, to have been imperfect; for, instead of taking his story direct from the original, he borrowed it in an adapted shape from a French melodrama.

The Neapolitans, up to this time, had not heard a note of Rossini's music. He had conquered the hearts of the Venetians and the Milanese. But he was unknown at Naples; and not to have earned the applause of the Neapolitan public was not to have achieved an Italian reputation. The connoisseurs of Naples were by no means disposed to accept Rossini on the strength of the success he had achieved at Milan and Venice; while the professors of the famous Conservatorio, whose classes he had not followed, were incredulous as to his being a composer of any sound musical learning, and were quite prepared to find him a much overrated man.

Rossini began by playing a trick on the Neapolitan audience; for in lieu of an original composition, he prefaced Elisabetta with an overture which he had written the year before at Milan for Aureliano in Palmira—and which he was to offer to the Romans a year afterwards as overture to Il Barbiere. The Neapolitans were delighted with the overture; but it has been surmised that had they known it to have been originally composed for an opera which had failed at Milan, they would not, perhaps, have applauded it so much. The first piece in the opera was, as Stendhal tells us, a duet for Leicester and his young wife, in the minor, which, says Stendhal, was "very original." The finale to the first act, in which the leading motives of the overture were introduced, called forth enthusiastic applause. "All the emotions of serious opera with no tedious intervals between:" such, Stendhal (or Carpani) informs us, was the phrase in which the general verdict of the Neapolitan public was expressed. Mademoiselle Colbran's greatest success, however, was not achieved until the second act where, on the rising of the curtain, Elisabetta, attired in an historical costume—warranted authentic and ordered expressly from London by a fanatical English admirer—had a grand scena. The concerted finale to this act was another triumph both for the composer and for the singers.

Elisabetta made but little mark beyond the frontiers of Italy. It contains much beautiful music; but the distribution of characters is not all that could be desired. Thus the parts of Norfolk, and of Leicester, are both given to tenors; though Norfolk as a wicked personage should have been represented by a baritone or bass. The bass singer, however, was still kept in the background; and at the San Carlo, though there were three admirable tenors— Davide, Nozzari, and Garcia,—there was no bass singer capable of taking a leading part. But for Rossini the bass singer might have remained indefinitely in obscurity. Gradually, however, he was brought to the front, not only in comic operas, where the Italians already tolerated him, but also in serious operas like Otello and Semiramide, and in half-character works such as Cenerentola and La Gazza Ladra. Elisabetta was the first Italian opera in which recitative was accompanied by the stringed quartet in place of the double bass and piano previously employed.

Rossini had plenty of work to do at Naples, for, besides composing two new operas every year he had to transpose parts and to correct and complete operatic scores. But in addition to all this he found time to write two works for Rome, which were produced in 1816, during the carnival. One of these, Torvaldo e Dorliska, was brought out at the Teatro Valle where it met with so little success that the composer informed his mother of the fact by sending her the drawing, not this time of a full-sized fiasco, but of a small fiasco or fiaschetto. Torvaldo e Dorliska, in which the principal parts were written for Remorini and Galli, the two best bass singers of their time, and for Donzelli, the celebrated tenor, must in spite of its failure have possessed some merit. It was performed at Paris in 1825 for the first appearance of Mademoiselle Garcia, the future Malibran; and Rossini borrowed from it the motive of the admirable letter duet in Otello.

CHAPTER VII

PREPARATIONS FOR THE BARBER

Torvaldo e Dorliska was followed, after but a short interval, by Il Barbiere, for which a contract was signed the very day, Dec. 26, on which Torvaldo was brought out. The contract was in the following terms:—

"Nobil Teatro di Torre Argentina, Dec. 26th, 1815.

"By the present act, drawn up privately between the parties, the value of which is not thereby diminished, and according to the conditions consented to by them, it has been stipulated as follows:—

"Signor Puca Sforza Cesarini, manager of the above-named theatre, engages Signor Maestro Gioachino Rossini for the next carnival season of the year 1816; and the said Rossini promises and binds himself to compose and produce on the stage, the second comic drama to be represented in the said season at the theatre indicated, and to the libretto which shall be given to him by the said manager, whether this libretto be old or new. The Maestro Rossini engages himself to deliver his score in the middle of the month of January, and to adapt it to the voices of the singers; obliging himself, moreover, to make, if necessary, all the changes which may be required, as much for the good execution of the music as to suit the capabilities or exigencies of the singers.

"The Maestro Rossini also promises and binds himself to be at Rome and to fulfil his engagement not later than the end of December of the current year, and to deliver to the copyist the first act of his opera, quite complete, on the 20th January, 1816. The 20th January is mentioned in order that the partial and general rehearsals may be commenced at once, and that the piece may be brought out the day the director wishes, the date of the first representation being hereby fixed for about the 5th of February. And the Maestro Rossini shall also deliver to the copyist, at the time wished, his second act, so that there may be time to make arrangements, and to terminate the rehearsals soon enough to go before the public on the evening mentioned above; otherwise the Maestro Rossini will expose himself to all losses, because so it must be and not otherwise.

"The Maestro Rossini shall, moreover, be obliged to direct his opera according to the custom, and to assist personally at all the vocal and orchestral rehearsals as many times as it shall be necessary, either at the theatre or elsewhere, at the will of the director; he obliges himself also to assist at the three first representations, to be given consecutively, and to direct the execution at the piano; and that because so it must be, and not otherwise. In reward for his fatigues the director engages to pay to the Maestro Rossini the sum and quantity of 400 Roman scudi, as soon as the first three representations which he is to direct at the piano shall be terminated.

"It is also agreed that in case of the piece being forbidden, or the theatre closed by the act of the authority, or for any unforeseen reason, the habitual practice in such cases, at the theatres of Rome and of all other countries shall be observed.

"And to guarantee the complete execution of this agreement, it shall be signed by the manager, and also by the Maestro Gioachino Rossini; and, in addition, the said manager grants lodgings to the Maestro Rossini during the term of the agreement, in the same house that is assigned to Signor Luigi Zamboni."

It is not certain, however, that Rossini received as much as 400 scudi (about 80l.) for his Barber, for Rossini, consulted long afterwards as to the correctness of the figures given in the contract, said he was under the impression that he had only received 300 scudi, or about 60l.[3] For the copyright of the music he received not a farthing. He did not even take the trouble to get it engraved; and two of the pieces, the overture (for which the overture to Elisabetta, previously known as the overture to Aureliano in Palmira, was afterwards substituted) and the scene of the music lesson (which Rossini had treated as a trio for the music-master, his pupil, and the pupil's guardian), were somehow lost in the theatre.

What the manager, on his side, purchased from Rossini, was the right of representation for two years; after which the work might be played by any one, as it might from the first moment be engraved by any one, without payment of any kind. The manuscript could not naturally find its way into the publisher's hands without the composer's consent. But as a matter of custom composers received nothing from the publishers. In England,

---

[3] M. Azevedo (G. Rossini, sa Vie et ses Œuvres, par A. Azevedo) says that "Rossini, consulted as to the correctness of these figures, thought there must be an error of 100 scudi. He was under the impression that he had only received 300 scudi for the Barber."

curiously enough, operatic composers have hitherto, with scarcely an exception, looked exclusively to the publishers for their profits, and have received nothing from the managers. The representation, according to the English view, serves to advertise the work, and to cause a demand at the music shops for the principal pieces. In Italy the engraved music did not apparently find many purchasers. The public cared above all things to hear the music executed on the stage; and with a view to the gratification of this desire the directors found it necessary to provide them constantly with new works, which they moreover found it necessary to order and to pay for.

The manager of the Argentina Theatre had experienced some trouble in procuring a suitable subject for the libretto he wished Rossini to set. The censorship was exercised with great severity, or rather with great scrupulosity, by the so-called Patriarch of Constantinople—Patriarchus in partibus infidelium and if, instead of Beaumarchais' Barber of Seville, Cesarini had proposed the same author's Marriage of Figaro, it is tolerably certain that the Patriarch would have refused to license so revolutionary a drama. When the politically harmless Barber of Seville was suggested, the censor at once approved. But it was now for Rossini to hesitate. To object, he had by the terms of his agreement no right; since he had undertaken to set any libretto that might be given to him, "new or old." The masters of the eighteenth century accepted readily for their operas themes which had been treated again and again, and even actual libretti to which, several times over, music had been composed. Almost every composer, for instance, had tried his hand on Dido Abandoned, or on the Descent of Orpheus into the Infernal

Regions; and we have seen that the story of Dido and the story of Orpheus were both treated by Rossini in his early days. Rossini, however, had now ideas of his own on the subject of musical setting, on the subject of dramatic propriety, and probably also on that of the propriety of taking for his theme one that had already been dealt with very successfully by a composer of high repute. Doubtless, in spite of his agreement, he would have refused altogether to take the Marriage of Figaro as subject of an opera, for we know by his recorded conversations with Ferdinand Hiller, that he regarded Mozart as the greatest of all dramatic composers. He felt, too, some delicacy, perhaps even some diffidence, in adopting the verses on which the illustrious Paisiello had already worked. He explained to Cesarini how impossible it would be for him to attack the identical libretto which Paisiello had set; and it was arranged that Sterbini, the poet who had furnished Rossini with the "words" (as musicians say),[4] of Torvaldo e Dorliska, should perform a like service for him in connection with the Barber. Sterbini and Rossini understood one another as librettist and composer always should do; and they lived together in the same house—"the house assigned to Luigi Zamboni," as the contract has it—until the work was finished. The admirable unity of the Barber, in which a person without previous information on the subject could scarcely say whether the words were written for the music or the music for the words, may doubtless in a great measure be accounted for by the fact that poet and musician

---

[4] A poet of our time, finding himself described on a title-page as the author of "words" which a composer had set to "music," suggested that, with a view to uniformity, for "music," "crotchets and quavers" should be substituted.

were always together during the composition of the opera; ready mutually to suggest and to profit by suggestions. Nor was it a slight advantage that the two operatic partners were living together "in the house assigned to Luigi Zamboni." Signor Luigi Zamboni was to take the part of Figaro; and we may be sure that "Largo al fattotum," set to music as soon as it was written, was handed to Zamboni as soon as it was composed.

Poet and composer had with them Beaumarchais' comedy of the Barber of Seville, and Paisiello's opera founded thereupon. Paisiello's opera was already known to Rossini, but he does not seem to have been quite familiar with Beaumarchais' comedy. Sterbini read it to him from beginning to end, and it was then decided what in Beaumarchais' comedy should be adopted—the principal dramatic scenes had of course to be taken—and what in Paisiello's libretto should be rejected. The queer incidental scenes for La Jeunesse who does nothing but sneeze, and L'Eveillé who does nothing but yawn, were cut out; and the work was so divided as to give Rossini the opportunity of composing a far greater number of musical pieces than are to be found in Paisiello's work. In dialogue scenes where Paisiello had contented himself with making the interlocutory personages exchange long passages of recitative, Rossini allowed the characters on the stage to declaim, but supported their declamation, not by a succession of chords, but by brilliant themes for the orchestra. No such thoroughly musical opera had before been composed. The series of melodies was almost continuous, and the characters on the stage only ceased to sing for tuneful strains to be executed by the instrumentalists. This transfer of the current of melody from the voices to the instruments was new in Italy; but brilliant examples of it are of course to be found in Mozart's operas which were performed for the first time in Italy, just before Rossini's Barber of Seville. Sterbini was a most accommodating poet. He was quite prepared to carry out the composer's ideas, and did not object to alter, curtail or add to his verses with a view to increasing the effectiveness of Rossini's music. After writing "Largo al fattotum," with the rapidity of an improvisator he handed the verses to Rossini, remarking—as Leopold II. remarked to Mozart with regard to the number of notes contained in the Seraglio— that there were "too many." "Precisely the right number," was virtually Rossini's reply; and inspired by their vivacity and their rhythmical flow, he, in fact, set them all. Something of the light-hearted elastic character of the constantly changing air must doubtless be attributed, not only to the verve with which Sterbini had written the words, but also to the impulsiveness and volubility with which Rossini knew beforehand that Zamboni would sing them.

Rossini worked so quickly that at times he found himself ahead of his poet—though, as regards the mere putting down on paper, the writing of verses is but trifling labour compared to that of composing music. Thus, without waiting for verses, he found a melody or devised a form for the next musical piece in the order agreed upon, and thereupon asked the obliging Sterbini to furnish him with suitable "words." Besides a leading singer in the next room, the poet and composer had by their side a number of copyists, to whom Rossini threw the sheets of music as he finished them. For thirteen days the joint authors had scarcely time to eat, and M. Azevedo asserts that they slept but little, and then only on a sofa, when it so happened that they could no longer keep their eyes open. For thirteen days Rossini did not shave; and when some one observed how strange it was that the Barber should have caused him to let his beard grow, he replied, that if he had shaved he should have gone out, and that if he had gone out he should not have returned as soon as he ought to have done. It seems incredible that in thirteen days the whole of the Barber should have been composed in score; but it is certain that the contract binding Rossini to compose it was only signed on the 26th December, and that he directed the first, second, and third performances of Torvaldo e Dorliska on the 27th, 28th and 29th. Some days, too, were lost in discussing various subjects for the proposed opera with the Roman censorship; and finally, when the Barber of Seville had been decided upon, Rossini had to read the comedy and to compare it with the libretto of Paisiello's opera, and to arrange with his own librettist a new distribution of scenes. The date of the first representation had been fixed for February 5th, and it was customary at the Italian theatres to allow fifteen days for rehearsals. He must then have finished the work in less than a month—between December 29th and January 24th; and one month is the time given by M. Castil-Blaze in his Histoire du Théâtre Italien. Stendhal, however, says (after Carpani) that the Barber was composed in thirteen days; and this statement is repeated—not, it must be presumed without verification—by M. Azevedo.

On one point connected with the production of the new Barber, Stendhal and Azevedo are quite at variance. According to the former, Rossini, as a matter of politeness, went through the unnecessary form of asking Paisiello's leave to reset the work, and received from him full permission to do so; the ancient master nourishing the hope that in recomposing a work which had already, as he believed, received its permanent musical form, the young composer would bring himself to grief. M. Azevedo denies that Rossini asked Paisiello's consent in the matter. But he adds that the venerable maestro knew of Rossini's intention, and not only looked forward to the failure of his youthful rival, but was even prepared to lend a helping hand thereto.

CHAPTER VIII

IL BARBIERE

ROSSINI did not bring out his Barber without addressing a few words of explanation, if not of apology, to the public; and by way of disclaiming all idea of entering into rivalry with Paisiello he announced his opera under a new title.

"Beaumarchais' comedy," he wrote, in an advertisement to the public, "entitled the Barber of Seville; or, The Useless Precaution,[5] is presented at Rome in the form of a comic drama, under the title of Almaviva; or, The Useless Precaution, in order that the public may be fully convinced of the sentiments of respect and veneration by which the author of the music of this drama is animated with regard to the celebrated Paisiello, who has already treated the subject under its primitive title.

"Himself invited to undertake this difficult task, the maestro, Gioachino Rossini, in order to avoid the reproach of entering into rivalry with the immortal author who preceded him, expressly required that the Barber of Seville should be entirely versified anew, and also that new situations should be added for the musical pieces, which, moreover, are required by the modern theatrical taste—entirely changed since the time when the renowned Paisiello wrote his work.

---

[5] In the Avvertimento al Pubblico the title of the comedy is given in Italian, "Il Barbiere di Sivigilia; ossia, L'Inutile Precauzione."

"Certain other differences between the arrangement of the present drama and that of the French comedy above-cited were produced by the necessity of introducing choruses, both for conformity with modern usage, and because they are indispensable for musical effect in so vast a theatre. The courteous public is informed of this beforehand, that it may also excuse the author of the new drama who, unless obliged by these imperious circumstances, would never have ventured to introduce the least change into the French work, already consecrated by the applause of all the theatres in Europe."

When, in the above announcement, Rossini speaks of "new situations for the musical pieces which are required by the modern theatrical taste, entirely changed since the time of Paisiello;" and again of the necessity of introducing choruses, "both for conformity with modern usage and because they are indispensable for musical effect in so vast a theatre," he describes changes which he himself introduced. The "modern theatrical taste" of Rossini's time was the taste he had himself created. That Paisiello's forms, and especially his formlessness (as in long scenes of recitative) were already considered old and were indeed obsolete, though his Barber had only been thirty-five years before the public, was implied rather pointedly in the sub-title of Sterbini's libretto, which was described as follows: "Comedy by Beaumarchais, newly versified throughout, and arranged for the use of the modern Italian Musical Theatre."

Paisiello's Barber had decidedly grown old. But as it was no longer played, people, by reason of its ancient reputation, continued to hold it in esteem; and the Roman public considered it very audacious for a young composer like Rossini to have ventured into competition with so illustrious a master. The young librettist Sterbini was considered quite as impertinent in his way as his musical associate. Among the Roman public a compact body of Paisiello's friends, with the spirit of Paisiello in the midst of them, formed a dangerous clique of enemies; and so determined was the opposition that Rossini had to meet on the occasion of his work being represented for the first time that the overture—an original work composed expressly for Il Barbiere, and not the overture to Aureliano and to Elisabetta afterwards substituted for it—was executed in the midst of a general murmuring; "such," remarks Zanolini, "as is heard on the approach of a procession."[6]

According to M. Azevedo the original overture was lost through the carelessness of a copyist; but the work could scarcely thus have disappeared unless not only the score, but also the band parts, had vanished. Stendhal says that the overture at the first representation was that of Aureliano in Palmira—the one performed even to the present day. He adds that the audience recognised, or fancied it recognised, in the overture the grumbling of the old guardian and the lively remonstrances of his interesting ward. However that may have been the overture was scarcely listened to; nor did the introduction meet with any better fate, nor, indeed, could even the appearance of Garcia on the stage dispose the public in favour of the new work.

Garcia, the most famous tenor of his time, was of course the Almaviva of the evening. It has already been seen that Luigi Zamboni, Rossini's fellow-lodger during the composition of the

---

[6] L'Ape Italiana. Paris 1836.

work, was the original Figaro. The Don Basilio was Vitarelli; Bartolo, Botticelli. The part of Rosina was assigned to Mme. Giorgi-Righetti, who has left a very interesting account of the first representation of the opera.[7]

The composer had been weak enough, says the prima donna of this historical evening, "to allow Garcia to sing beneath Rosina's balcony a Spanish melody of his own arrangement." Garcia held that as the scene was laid in Spain, and as Count Almaviva was a Spaniard nothing could be more appropriate than that this interesting personage should address the lady of his heart in Spanish song. Unfortunately he forgot to tune his guitar, and this indispensable preliminary operation had to be performed by Rosina's serenader on the stage. The public began to laugh; then a string broke, and the public began to hiss. When the broken string had been replaced, and the air so awkwardly prefaced was at length heard, the public did not like it and only listened to it enough to be able to reproduce certain passages of it in burlesque tones. The introduction to Figaro's air, which, as every opera-goer knows, is, before being sung by the vocalist, played by the orchestra, attracted, as well it might do, a certain amount of attention. When, however, Zamboni entered with another guitar, the anti-guitarists set up a loud laugh, and without waiting to see whether the baritone, unlike the tenor, had taken the trouble to tune his instrument beforehand, hissed and hooted so that not a note of "Largo al Fattotum" was heard. When Mme. Giorgi-Righetti made her appearance in the balcony, she was, in her character of favourite singer, applauded; but having no air assigned to her in this not very suitable situation, the audience

---

[7] Cenn di una donna già contante sopra il maestro Rossini.

thought they were being robbed of the expected cavatina, and uttered murmurs of disapprobation. The brilliant and melodious duet for Almaviva and Figaro was sung in the midst of hisses and derisive shouts. When, however, Rosina reappeared and sang the first notes of "Una voce" the audience became silent; a chance was given to the composer for the sake of the singer. Mme. Giorgi-Righetti was radiant with youth and beauty; the effect of her fresh, beautiful voice was too much for the opposition. The conclusion of her bright, sparkling air was followed by three long rounds of applause. Rossini bowed from his place, at the head of the orchestra, to the public, and then turning towards the singer, whispered, "Oh natura!"

Vitarelli, the representative of Don Basilio, had "made up" admirably for the part; and his entry would possibly have been effective but that a trap having been left open on the stage he stumbled over it, fell, damaged his face, and on rising had to begin his admirable dramatic air on the efficacy of calumny with his handkerchief to his nose. A portion of the public is said to have imagined that the fall, the injuries to the face, the handkerchief to the nose, were all in the business of the part, and thinking it savoured of buffoonery, expressed their disapproval accordingly. The duet of the letter was objected to by reason of certain incidents afterwards left out; but the music must have been liked for its own sake had it only been heard. As if the untuned guitar, the broken string, the newly-placed cavatina, the open trap, the fall of Don Basilio, and the necessity under which Rosina's music-master found himself of singing "La Calunnia" with a handkerchief in front of his mouth had not been enough, the opening of the finest concerted finale which had yet been given to the Italian stage was the signal for the appearance of a cat, which was chased in one direction by Figaro, in another by Bartholo, and which, in a wild endeavour to escape from an attack made upon it by Basilio, ran into the skirt of Rosina's dress. The self-introduction of the cat among the principal characters, grouped together for the finely built concerted piece which brings the first act to an end, disarranged as a matter of course all the master's combinations. During the performance of the opening movement the attention of the public was concentrated entirely on the cat, and general laughter went on increasing until the long, elaborate, constantly varied, and, on all other occasions, highly interesting finale was brought to an end.

With something like a just appreciation of his own merit and with profound contempt for the injustice and insolence of the public, Rossini, on the fall of the curtain, turned round and applauded. He was the only person in the theatre who did so; and the audience indignant at the presumption of this interested minority of one, was at the same time so astonished that it forgot at the time to manifest its resentment.

The moment of vengeance arrived when the curtain rose for the second act. The public showed what it thought of Rossini's having ventured to show what he thought of his own music, by hissing and hooting in such a manner that not a note of the second act was heard. The composer, while this organised noise was being kept up, remained perfectly calm at the orchestral piano. At the end of the performance he went home to bed; and when the principal singers called upon him soon afterwards to condole with him he was fast asleep.

The only change that Rossini next day found it necessary to make in his work was to substitute a new air for the unfortunate Spanish song which Garcia had been allowed to introduce. This gave him no trouble. He simply transcribed for the solo voice the melody of the celebrated chorus which had already figured first in Ciro in Babilonia, and afterwards in Aureliano in Palmira. Such was the origin of the beautiful "Ecco ridente il cielo" which he handed to Garcia as he wrote it, and which was sung the same evening. Those who believe in the absolute significance of music apart from words, may be interested to hear that Almaviva's charming love song was, as first composed, a prayer—as a love song after all may well be.

At the second representation the Barber was comparatively well received. Being heard, it was naturally admired. Indeed, a certain number of connoisseurs are said to have appreciated it from the very first, though on the opening night the difficulty must have been not to understand the work—which appeals alike to the simplest, and to the most cultivated, musical intelligence—but merely to hear it. After a few performances Rossini's new work began to excite enthusiasm; and it had not been before the public for more than a week when it was received nightly with frantic applause.

Garcia's Spanish melody was, after some years, reintroduced into the Barber by Rubini; the trio which, in the music lesson scene, occupied the place now filled by no matter what fancy air that the Rosina of the evening thinks fit to introduce, is known to have been lost: and it has been seen that, according to some authorities, a like fate attended the overture written specially for the work. Stendhal, on the unacknowledged authority of

Carpani, states that at the first representation the opera was preceded by the overture to Aureliano in Palmira and to Elisabetta, which, though heard in connection with the former work at Milan and in connection with the latter at Naples, had never been heard at Rome. Besides borrowing from himself, Rossini, in more than one "number" of the Barber of Seville, was indebted to the invention of others. The melody of the trio "Zitti zitti" is taken, note for note, from Simon's air in Haydn's Seasons—a work, it will be remembered, of which Rossini in his early youth had directed the performance at the Lyceum of Bologna. The very lively tune sung by the Duenna Berta is adapted without much alteration from a Russian dance, which Rossini had heard played by a Russian lady of his acquaintance. It soon became the custom not to listen to Berta's air, which is always assigned to an inferior singer; and it acquired the name of the "Ice tune;" not in allusion to its place of origin, but because, during its performance, the people in the boxes called for ices. The part of Rosina, which in the present day is usually given to the soprano, was composed for the mezzo-soprano voice. Mme. Giorgi-Righetti sang it, of course, in its original key; that of F. Many a soprano has sung it in G. According to an account given by M. Castil-Blaze in his Histoire du Théâtre Italien of the different keys in which the principal airs of Il Barbiere have been sung, Figaro's "Largo al fattotum," written for Zamboni in the key of C, is generally sung in B flat; Tamburini, however, sang it in B natural. Basilio's "La calunnia," written in D, is for the most part sung in C. Lablache used to sing in D flat the air for Bartholo, written in E flat.

Whatever may be said as to the character belonging absolutely to this or that key, it would be difficult to allow that the music of Rosina, of Figaro, of Basilio, or of Bartolo has either lost or gained by these frequent transpositions.

CHAPTER IX

ROSSINI AND THE COMIC IN MUSIC

NO composer has written more lively, more graceful comedy music than Rossini. But, except Il Figlio per Azzardo, with its high notes for low voices, its low voices for high notes, its ludicrous accompaniments, and its grotesque instruments of percussion in the shape of metal lamp-shades tapped with violin bows, Rossini never wrote music which, comic or serious, was not charming; and Il Figlio per Azzardo was nothing but a practical joke played for the benefit of an unreasonable and impolite manager. It may be interesting to consider in what the musical comic really consists.

The æsthetics of music have been much neglected; and no one, so far as I know, has yet attempted to explain or even to define the comic in music. Everything, it may be roughly said, is comic that makes one laugh; and if this be the case, then, between comic music and music so utterly bad as to be ludicrous and absurd, there should be no great difference. The intention, however, of the composer must count for something, and one cannot accept as comic music which is simply played or sung very much out of tune. Many persons disbelieve altogether in comic music. Lively, brilliant music is admirable, and commends itself to every taste. But comic music is for the most part as objectionable as comic women, than which nothing much more objectionable can well be imagined. It is the province of music to charm, to fascinate, to call up visions of delight, but not to cause fits of laughter. It may be questioned, moreover, whether laughter, or even the least tendency to laugh, can be provoked by music, so long as it is composed and executed according to the rules of art. A comic poem, a comic picture, may be a masterpiece of artistic expression, but it is difficult to imagine a perfect musical composition which would afford matter for merriment. Gounod's Funeral March for a Marionette is a graceful, melodious piece of music, in which there is nothing comic but the title. No one would find it in the slightest degree amusing but for the description of the incidents it is supposed to illustrate, which is usually printed in the programmes of concerts where the said funeral march is to be performed. In the old-fashioned Italian operas of the buffo type there are plenty of chattering songs in which the humour, such as it is, consists in the words being uttered so rapidly that any greater rapidity of utterance would seem to be impossible. Here some little amusement may be caused by witnessing the efforts of the buffo singer or singers—for there are often two or three of them chattering at once—to overcome such difficulties as have been deliberately put forward for that purpose by the composer. If this, however, be humour, it is humour of a very mean order, on a par with that of "Peter Piper pecked a peck of pepper," and other verbal devices for testing the power of a speaker to speak rapidly and at the same time distinctly. In Paisiello's Barber of Seville there was a comic piece for two fantastic and quite episodical characters, borrowed from Beaumarchais' comedy (where, as already mentioned, Rossini took good care to leave them), of whom one, La Jeunesse, sneezed, while the other, L'Eveillé, yawned, in the presence of old Bartolo. It may be very funny to sneeze and to yawn, but such fun as therein lies can scarcely be said to be of a musical character.

Much, indeed, that is considered comic in music possesses the same sort of drollery that belongs in comic writing to grammatical errors, or to mistakes in spelling. Romberg's Toy Symphony, in which, with the usual orchestral basis, solo instruments of a burlesque character, such as the rattle, the penny trumpet, the child's drum, and so on, are from time to time introduced, is surprisingly funny. But with the first feeling of surprise the fun also vanishes; for the humour in this, as in all other toy symphonies, consists only in giving good music to bad instruments. If Romberg's symphony were played throughout with instruments of the best make in the parts written for the "toys," no one not previously acquainted with the work would imagine for a moment that it was intended to be amusing. In Mozart's Musical Joke, again, the joke consists in the instruments coming in at wrong places, executing inappropriate phrases, and playing out of tune. There are elements of beauty in the work, as in everything that Mozart composed; but the humour of the piece is akin to that of those American humourists of whom one of the most remarkable was not ashamed to complain of "Mr. Chaucer" that he could not spell. A composer may easily produce a laugh if he will only condescend to an absurdity so easy to realise, by causing a pretentious introduction to be followed by a trivial tune; or he may produce a genuine burlesque effect by imitating with characteristic exaggeration the style of some other composer; or he may show a certain wit by means of musical allusions, as Mozart has done in the supper scene of Don Giovanni, where Don Juan's private band is made to play "Non più andrai," in order that Leporello may refer to the fact of its not having been quite appreciated when it was first heard. But without Leporello's spoken (or declaimed) words it would occur to no one that there was anything amusing in introducing into one opera an air from another.

Of the music suitable to comedy Rossini was undoubtedly a master; and in such music the Barber of Seville abounds. But though the most characteristic air in the whole opera, Figaro's "Largo al fattotum," is bright, gay, joyful, impulsive, one cannot say that it is comic. Heard for the first time apart from the words, it would cause no one to laugh, nor even, except as the expression of musical satisfaction, to smile.

Rossini could write very comic music indeed when he pleased. He knew well enough, however, that he was writing bad music at the time. He launched into all sorts of extravagances, and introduced some effects in which, as we have already seen, musical instruments, properly so called, had no part.

Meyerbeer, in his highly but sometimes almost grotesque orchestral effects, has approached the very verge of burlesque music such as Rossini, in the little opera referred to, deliberately wrote. The simple motive, for instance, of the march in Robert le Diable is given, when introduced for the first time, to four kettledrums. A four-note melody executed on four kettledrums would in a burlesque have excited roars of laughter. Jessica was "never merry when she heard sweet music." But sweet music is one thing, and grotesque music another. It is easier, indeed, to speak of comic music than to define it accurately, or to cite specimens that will bear analysis.

CHAPTER X

FROM "OTELLO" TO "SEMIRAMIDE"

IN 1816, Rossini brought out at the San Carlo, of Naples, the second of his serious operas, or at least the second of those which were destined to make a mark: Otello. This work exhibited reforms of various kinds much more important than any that are to be noticed in Tancredi. Recitative is more sparingly used than in the earlier work, and for the first time it is accompanied by the full band. Now, too, Rossini banished the piano from the orchestra, where it had been allowed to remain long after its expulsion as an orchestral instrument from the bands of Germany and (thanks to Gluck) of France. Two years after its production at Naples Byron witnessed a representation of Otello at Venice, and gives some account of it in one of his letters dated 1818. The libretto struck him as bad and ridiculous, but he praises the music, and the style in which it was executed. Lord Mount-Edgcumbe, when the work was given in London, must have been disgusted to find two of the leading parts assigned to bass voices. Iago is of necessity almost as important a character as Othello himself. Rossini's librettist kept him, nevertheless, a little too much in the back ground, while Roderigo, on the other hand, is too much brought forward. In expelling the piano from the orchestra Rossini at the same time, did away with those interminable recitatives accompanied by piano or piano and double bass which separated the musical pieces in the works composed by Rossini's predecessors. It was the impersonation, however, of Otello by Davide, which, in the way of acting and singing, helped more than anything else to ensure the success of the performance.

"Davide," wrote a French critic, M. Bertin, from Venice, in 1823, "excites among the dilettanti of this town an enthusiasm and delight which could scarcely be conceived without having been witnessed. He is a singer of the new school, full of mannerism, affectation and display, abusing, like Martin, his magnificent voice with its prodigious compass (three octaves comprised between four B flats). He crushes the principal motive of an air beneath the luxuriance of his ornamentation, which has no other merit than that of difficulty conquered. But he is also a singer of warmth, verve, expression, energy and musical sentiment; alone he can fill up and give life to a scene; it is impossible for another singer to carry away an audience as he does, and when he will only be simple he is admirable; he is the Rossini of song, he is a great singer, the greatest I have ever heard. Doubtless the manner in which Garcia plays and sings the part of Otello is preferable, taking it altogether, to that of Davide. It is purer, more severe, more constantly dramatic; but with all his faults Davide produces more effect—a great deal more effect. There is something in him, I cannot say what, which, even when he is ridiculous, commands, enhances attention. He never leaves you cold, and when he does not move you he astonishes you; in a word, before hearing him, I did not know what the power of singing really was. The enthusiasm he excites is without limits. In fact his faults are not faults, for Italians who in their opera seria do not employ what the French call the tragic style, scarcely understand us when we tell them that a waltz or a quadrille movement is out of place in the mouth of a Cæsar, an Assur, or an Otello. With them the essential thing is to please; they are only difficult on this point, and their indifference as to all the rest is really inconceivable. Here is an example of it. Davide, considering, apparently, that the final duet of Otello did not sufficiently show off his voice, determined to substitute for it a duet from Armida ('Amor possente nome') which is very pretty, but anything rather than severe. As it was impossible to kill Desdemona to such a tune, the Moor, after giving way to the most violent jealousy, sheaths his dagger, and begins in the most tender and graceful manner his duet with Desdemona, at the conclusion of which he takes her politely by the hand, and retires amidst the applause and bravos of the public, who seems to think it quite natural that the piece should finish in this manner, or rather that it should not finish at all; for after this beautiful dénouement the action is about as far advanced as it was in the first scene. We do not in France carry our love of music so far as to tolerate such absurdities as these, and perhaps we are right."

Otello in the present day seems somewhat antiquated, and in some of the dramatic scenes the accent of passion is smothered beneath roulades and vocalistic ornaments of all kinds. But it contains some fine pieces, and the last act is full of beauty. Speaking once to a friend on the subject of his own operas, Rossini said that much of what he had written must in time pass out of fashion, but that he believed the second act of William Tell, the last act of Otello, and the whole of the Barber of Seville would survive the rest.[8] Il Barbiere is, indeed, as fresh now as when it was first written. Yet Paisiello's treatment of the same

---

[8] M. de Saint-George, in a speech he delivered at Rossini's funeral.

subject was found to be old-fashioned in a very few years—was in fact rendered so by the newness, the brightness, the youthful gaiety of Rossini's setting.

Nothing more need be said in this volume of Rossini considered as a composer of comic opera. He cultivated every style, including the ancient style of La Cenerentola which contains much comic with some serious music, and of La Gazza Ladra, which might well have been treated seriously throughout, though in some of the gravest situations of this work he is gay, in some of the severest, lively.

La Cenerentola, like Il Barbiere, La Gazza Ladra, and so many successful operas by Rossini and other Italian composers (L'Elisir, Linda, Lucrezia, La Favorita, Maria di Rohan, for instance, of Donizetti, and the Sonnambula and Norma of Bellini), is based on a French play—the ingenious comedy of Cendrillon, by Etienne. Rossini composed it for the Teatro Valle of Rome, where it was produced for the carnival of 1817, on the 26th of December, 1816, precisely one year after Torvaldo e Dorliska, nearly one year after the Barber, a few months after Otello, and a few months before La Gazza Ladra. Between the winter of 1815 and the spring of 1816, Rossini composed and produced six operas, including the four admirable ones just named. The two others given with comparatively little success were Torvaldo e Dorliska and La Gazzetta.

La Cenerentola, on its first production, excited no such enthusiasm as Il Barbiere, but drew after its second or third representation. It is known to have been Rossini's custom when an opera of his fell, to pick up the pieces; and the score of La

Cenerentola was adorned throughout with fragments saved from the ruins of his earlier works; such as the wholly forgotten Pietra del Paragone and the never-much-remembered Turco in Italia. To the former had originally belonged the drinking chorus, the burlesque proclamation of the Baron, and the duet "Un soave non so chè;" to the latter the duet "Zitti zitti," the sestet and the stretta of the finale.

To La Cenerentola belongs the most beautiful and the most striking of Rossini's final airs for the prima donna: the once highly popular "Non più mesta." This was his fourth air of the kind; and he now abandoned this method of bringing an opera to a brilliant termination in favour of other composers—who duly adopted it.

The part of Cenerentola, like that of Rosina, was written for Madame Giorgi-Righetti, who obtained therein the most brilliant success, especially in the famous rondo finale. All Rossini's great prima-donna parts were composed for the contralto or for the mezzo-soprano voice; for Madame Marcolini, Tancredi; for Madame Giorgi-Righetti, Rosina and Cenerentola; and for Mademoiselle Colbran, Desdemona and Semiramide. When Rossini began his career, so absurd was the prevalent custom of distributing the parts that the first woman's part was habitually given to the contralto, the first man's part to the sopranist, or artificial male soprano. Rossini continued to compose principal female parts, first for the contralto, then for the mezzo-soprano voice; and it was only when he produced Matilda di Shubrun towards the end of his Italian career (1821) that he assigned a leading character to a soprano. Matilda in Matilda di Shubrun, and Matilde in Guillaume Tell, are the only two parts that Rossini ever wrote for the soprano voice.

Whether soprano voices have been forced into activity in order to suit new tastes, or whether composers have taken to writing for the soprano voice because in the present day sopranos, and especially "light sopranos," abound, whereas good mezzo-soprano and contralto voices are but rarely to be met with, it would be difficult to say. But with the exception of Meyerbeer's Africaine and Donizetti's Favorita, no leading operatic part has for the last fifty years or more been written for the contralto voice.

A new kind of part, however, has been found for the most masculine of feminine voices; such parts as those of Pippo in La Gazza Ladra, of Malcolm Græme in La Donna del Lago, and of Arsace in Semiramide; and here again we see an innovation of Rossini's, which by his successors has been generally adopted.

In connection with La Gazza Ladra a few words may here be said of Rossini's orchestration; much more varied, more brilliant and more sonorous than that of his predecessors. Rossini introduced new instruments, and with them new instrumental combinations. These innovations, like those consisting in a new distribution of the voice parts, and in the substitution of orchestral melodies with declamatory phrases here and there for the singers in lieu of endless recitative accompanied by chords for the violoncello and piano, excited the hostility of many orthodox professors, together with old-fashioned connoisseurs and amateurs of all kinds. They accused Rossini of bringing clarinets from cowherds, horns from the hunting field, trumpets from the camp, and trombones from the infernal regions. He was destined, on establishing himself at Paris, to introduce cornets, ophicleides, and, in the overture to William Tell, the nearest possible approach to the instrument with which the cowherds of Switzerland do really appeal to the animals placed under their care. But before he had reached these extremes, before he had in Semiramide brought an entire military band on to the stage, and had in the same opera written for four horns a beautiful and beautifully harmonised melody which does not in any way suggest the chase, he raised the mortal anger of one of his adversaries and actually placed his life in danger by beginning the overture to La Gazza Ladra with a duet for drums. A young enthusiast on the side of stagnation went about armed with the proclaimed intention of slaying the ruthless innovator. Rossini sent for the juvenile fanatic, talked to him, explained that in a piece of a military character drums were not altogether out of place and at last succeeded in appeasing his fury.

To appreciate at a glance Rossini's importance as a writer for the orchestra it is only necessary to recall the fact that he alone of Italian composers has composed overtures which live with a life of their own apart from the works to which they belong, and that of such overtures he has left five; those of the Barber, of La Gazza Ladra, of Semiramide, of the Siege of Corinth, and of William Tell.

CHAPTER XI

ROSSINI ON HIS TRAVELS

WHEN in 1823, the year of Semiramide's being produced at Venice, Rossini started with his wife, the former Mdlle. Colbran, for Paris—whence he made his way to London, returning to Paris soon afterwards—he enjoyed a world-wide reputation, but was far from being rich. Thanks, however, to a season in London, and to five years' residence in Paris, where lucrative posts were given to him, he soon made his fortune.

Speaking some thirty years afterwards of his visit to London, Rossini said to Hiller:[9] "'From the beginning I had an opportunity of observing how disproportionately singers were paid in comparison with composers. If the composer got fifty ducats, the singer received a thousand. Italian operatic composers might formerly write heaven knows how many operas, and yet only be able to exist miserably. Things hardly went otherwise with myself until my appointment under Barbaja.'

"'Tancredi was your first opera which really made a great hit, maestro; how much did you get for it?'

"'Five hundred francs,' replied Rossini, 'and when I wrote my

---

[9] "Conversations with Rossini," by Ferdinand Hiller. Musical World, 1856.

last Italian opera, Semiramide, and stipulated for 5,000 francs, I was looked upon, not by the impresario alone, but by the entire public, as a kind of pickpocket.'

"'You have the consolation of knowing,' said Hiller, 'that singers, managers, and publishers, have been enriched by your means.'

"'A fine consolation' replied Rossini. 'Except during my stay in England, I never gained sufficient by my art to enable me to put by anything; and even in London I did not get money as a composer, but as an accompanist.'

"'But still,' observed Hiller,'that was because you were a celebrated composer.'

"'That is what my friends said,' replied Rossini, 'to decide me to do it. It may have been prejudice, but I had a kind of repugnance to being paid for accompanying on the piano, and I have only done so in London. However, people wanted to see the tip of my nose, and to hear my wife. I had fixed for our co-operation at musical soirées the tolerably high price of 50l. We attended somewhere about sixty such soirées, and that was after all worth having. In London, too, musicians will do anything to get money, and some delicious facts came under my observation there. For instance, the first time that I undertook the task of accompanist at a soirée of this description, I was informed that Puzzi, the celebrated horn-player, and Dragonetti, the more celebrated contrabassist, would also be present. I thought they would perform solos; not a bit of it! They were to assist me in accompanying. "Have you then your parts to accompany these pieces?" I asked them. "Not we," was their answer, "but we get well paid, and we accompany as we think fit!"

'"These extemporaneous attempts at instrumentation struck me as rather dangerous, and I therefore begged Dragonetti to content himself with giving a few pizzicatos when I winked at him, and Puzzi to strengthen the final cadenzas with a few notes, which, being a good musician, he easily invented for the occasion. In this manner things went off without any very disastrous results, and every one was pleased."'

"'Delicious!' exclaimed Hiller, 'still it strikes me that the English have made great progress in a musical point of view. At the present time a great deal of good music is performed in London—it is well performed and listened to attentively, that is to say, at public concerts. In private drawing-rooms music still plays a sorry part, and a great number of individuals, totally devoid of talent, give themselves airs of incredible assurance, and impart instruction on subjects of which their knowledge amounts almost to nothing.'

'"I knew in London a certain professor who had amassed a large fortune as a teacher of singing and the pianoforte,' said Rossini, 'while all he understood was to play a little, most wretchedly, on the flute. There was another man, with an immense connection, who did not even know the notes. He employed an accompanist to beat into his head the pieces he afterwards taught, and to accompany him in his lessons; but he had a good voice."'

Many of the French composers, with about an equal proportion of critics, received Rossini with anything but cordiality. He was chiefly condemned as a seeker after new effects. But Berlioz some years later vituperated him from quite another point of view. He found his music heartless, unemotional, and written entirely for the singer, and for the sake of vocal, to the disregard of dramatic effect. "If," he afterwards said, "it had been in my power to place a barrel of powder under the Salle Louvois and blow it up during the representation of La Gazza Ladra or Il Barbiere, with all that it contained, I certainly should not have failed to do so."

The composer Bertin, less a contemporary than a predecessor of Rossini, wrote of him in the following terms:—

"M. Rossini has a brilliant imagination, verve, originality, great fecundity; but he knows that he is not always pure and correct; and, whatever certain persons may say, purity of style is not to be disdained, and faults of syntax are never excusable. Besides, since the writers of our daily journals constitute themselves judges in music, having qualified myself by Montano, Le Délire, Aline, &c., I think I have the right to give my opinion ex professo. I give it frankly, and sign it, which is not done by certain persons who strive incognito to make and unmake reputations. All this has been suggested only by the love of art, and in the interest of M. Rossini himself. This composer is beyond contradiction the most brilliant talent that Italy has produced since Cimarosa; but one may deserve to be called celebrated without being on an equality with Mozart."

It seems afterwards to have occurred to Bertin that music as good as Rossini's might be composed by machinery. He declares, indeed, in a pamphlet directed against Rossini, entitled "La musique mechanique et de la musique philosophique," that he once asked Maelzel, the inventor of the metronome, whether he could construct a machine to compose music; upon which

Maelzel daringly replied that he could, but that his mechanically-made tunes would not be up to the level of Sacchini, Cimarosa, and Mozart, and would be worthy only of Rossini.

"M. Auber has told me," says M. Jouvin, in his Life of that composer, "how he met Rossini for the first time at a dinner given by Carafa in honour of his illustrious compatriot. On rising from table the maestro, at the request of his host, went to the piano and sang Figaro's cavatina, 'Largo al fattotum della città.'

"'I shall never forget,' said M. Auber to me, 'the effect produced by his lightning-like execution.' Rossini had a beautiful baritone voice, and he sang his music with a spirit and verve which neither Pellegrini nor Galli nor Lablache approached in the same part. As for his art as an accompanist, it was marvellous; it was not on a key-board but on an orchestra that the vertiginous hands of the pianist seemed to gallop. When he had finished I looked mechanically at the ivory keys; I fancied I could see them smoking. On arriving home I felt much inclined to throw my scores into the fire. 'It will warm them, perhaps,' I said to myself; 'besides, what is the use of composing music, if one cannot compose like Rossini?'"

Apart from a little professional jealousy, Rossini met in Paris with the warmest possible reception; and the men in authority gave him substantial marks of their esteem. He was appointed director of the Théâtre des Italiens, with a salary of 20,000 francs a year; and when after eighteen months' service he resigned this post, the salary was continued to him in connection with another, of which the duties were purely nominal: that of "Inspector of singing." In granting Rossini this salary, the object of the government was to induce him to remain in France, and to compose a series of works for the Académie where, after producing Il Viaggio a Reims, at the Italian Theatre in honour of Charles X.'s coronation, he brought out in succession Le Siège de Corinthe,[10] re-arranged from Maometto Secundo, an opera of the year 1820; Moïse, re-arranged from Mosè in Egitto, a Lenten opera oratorio of the year 1818; Le Comte Ory, re-arranged with many additions from Il Viaggio a Reims; and his greatest work Guillaume Tell.

Every one knows that after William Tell, Rossini wrote no more for the stage. But every one does not know that he for some little time afterwards entertained an idea of composing an opera on the subject of Faust. "Yes," answered Rossini, when Ferdinand Hiller questioned him on the subject, "it was for a long period a favourite notion of mine, and I had already planned the whole scenarium with Jouy; it was naturally based upon Goethe's poem. At this time, however there arose in Paris a regular 'Faust' mania; every theatre had a particular 'Faust' of its own, and this somewhat damped my ardour. Meanwhile the revolution of July had taken place; the Grand Opera, previously a royal institution, passed into the hands of a private person; my mother was dead, and my father found life in Paris unbearable because he did not understand French: so I cancelled the agreement which bound me by rights to send in four other grand operas, preferring to remain quietly in my native land, enlivening the last years of my

---

[10] Le Siège de Corinthe was the first opera—it was the thirty sixth he had composed—that Rossini sold to a music publisher.

old father's existence. I had been far away from my poor mother when she expired; this was an endless source of regret to me, and I was most apprehensive that the same thing might occur in my father's case."

Many explanations have been given of Rossini's reasons for abstaining from writing any more for the stage, when he had once produced William Tell—nor did he afterwards compose anything whatever of importance except his thoroughly beautiful Stabat Mater. Some of these explanations have been already referred to. The truth in this matter seems to have been that Rossini acted under the influence of a great variety of reasons. Without being hurt by the comparative coldness with which William Tell for a time was received, without being jealous of Meyerbeer's and of Halévy's success, which, according to some anecdote-mongers, caused him to exclaim: "Je reviendrai quand les Juifs auront fini leur Sabbat," without even having "written himself out," he may well have reflected whether such a strain as he had subjected himself to in composing William Tell was worth undergoing a second time. With the exception of Il Viaggio a Reims nothing that he wrote for Paris, until he undertook William Tell, was absolutely new. He had already lost the habit, if not the faculty, of composing rapidly; and this same Viaggio a Reims was the only original work he produced between Semiramide, 1823, and Guillaume Tell, 1829. Writing at Paris for as fine an orchestra as that of the San Carlo Theatre, and for a finer chorus, he paid particular attention to the choral and orchestral portions of his last great work. He also profited by the fact that at the Académie he was free to have as many rehearsals as he pleased; and to turn this advantage to the greatest possible account he gave himself infinite, and with him quite unusual pains, to secure a perfect execution of his opera. In writing for the voices moreover, he had completely changed his style. What indeed can be more different from the florid and frequently insignificant,—or, so to say, anti-significant— passages in the rich, soft, voluptuous melodies of Semiramide, than the simple, emotional, eminently dramatic strains given to the singers in Guillaume Tell? Heine speaks in his "Parisian Letters" of Meyerbeer's mother having once told him that her son was "not obliged to compose;" on which Heine remarks that a windmill might as well say it was not "obliged" to go round: though a windmill will turn if the wind blows, just as a composer will produce music if moved by the spirit. Talking on this most interesting subject of speculation to Ferdinand Hiller, Rossini himself confessed that "when a man has composed thirty-seven operas he begins to feel a little tired." Guillaume Tell, in any case, marks the end of Rossini's career as an operatic composer.

Opera has a distinct history in Italy, in France, and in Germany. For a considerable time it makes progress in Italy. Then Italian composers and Italian singers go abroad taking Italian opera with them. German composers, too, visit Italy, and after studying there return to their native land, to produce with modifications operas which must still be regarded as Italian in character. At last the Germans who have studied in Italy become the rivals of the Italian masters. Then Gluck and Piccinni contend with one another in presence of French audiences, and above all, of French critics. Finally it becomes the turn of the Italians to borrow from the Germans; for Mozart, so highly indebted for his melodic inspiration—or at least for his melodic forms—to Italy, was so much before the Italians in regard to the composition of his orchestra and the construction of his musical pieces, that when Rossini wished to introduce into Italian opera the important reforms which must always be associated with his name, he had nothing to do but to turn to Mozart as a model. Rossini was the first Italian composer who accompanied recitative with the full band, assigned leading parts to bass singers, made of each dramatic scene one continuous piece of music, and brought to perfection those highly varied, amply developed concerted finales, which form so striking a feature in modern Italian opera. All these innovations were simply adaptations from Mozart.

The history of Rossini's Italian career is the history of opera in Italy during the first half of the nineteenth century; for Rossini caused the works of his predecessors to be laid aside, while his own works and those of his immediate successors, and in an artistic sense followers, continued to be played almost to the exclusion of all others until the Verdi period. And even Verdi, who in his latter works has studied dramatic consistency and dramatic effect more than Rossini studied them in his earlier works, must be regarded as belonging, more or less completely, to the school of Rossini.

CHAPTER XII

DONIZETTI AND BELLINI

DONIZETTI, Rossini's immediate successor but not supplanter, composed from sixty to seventy operas ("c'est beaucoup" dirait Candide) of which to this day three at least ("c'est beaucoup" dirait Martin), are still played regularly every season in London: Lucia, Lucrezia, and La Favorita. Of his two charming works in the light style—comic operas in which the composer never approaches the farcical, never once ceases to be graceful— neither L'Elisir nor Don Pasquale can be compared to the much more vigorous Barber. Nor has Donizetti produced any work so full of melody as Semiramide, or so dramatic as William Tell. But he rises to unwonted heights in the last act of La Favorite; which, composed for the French Académie, became naturalised in due time on the Italian operatic stage under the title of La Favorita.

Although the career of Donizetti was very much longer than that of Bellini, whom he preceded and whom he survived, he produced in proportion to the number of his works fewer by a great deal which have kept the stage.

Donizetti brought out his first opera Enrico di Borgogna at Venice in 1818, when he was twenty years of age, and Catarina Cornaro, his sixty-third (not to count two or three that were never produced) at Naples, in 1844, when he was forty-six.

Bellini brought out the first of his works performed in public, Bianca e Fernando (he had previously composed a sort of pasticcio for the school theatre of the Naples Conservatorio) at the San Carlo in 1826, when he was twenty-five years of age; and his last, I Puritani, at Paris in 1835. He had a career then, of but nine years, during which he composed ten operas, of which five were played with great success, and of which three, La Sonnambula, Norma, and I Puritani, forty-five years after their composer's death, still keep the stage. Stendhal (or perhaps it was Carpani) had foretold that Rossini, the composer of florid music, would be followed by a master whose melodies would be remarkable for extreme simplicity, and this prophecy was fulfilled in the case of Bellini.

Donizetti, like so many other composers, was not encouraged by his parents to adopt the career in which he was destined to obtain so much distinction. When, however, his father at last consented to his becoming a professional musician, he is said to have presented him with an ivory scraper, as if to impress upon him the necessity of practising the art of erasing. Probably no composer ever did less in that line than Donizetti; and though he wrote more accurately than many other Italian composers, one is frequently astonished to find in his works melodies of significance and beauty followed at haphazard by the merest trivialities. Donizetti never went to work without the paternal scraper by his side. The fluent composer, however, had no occasion to make use of it for scratching out notes; and it never seems to have occurred to him to strike out feeble passages, not to say entire pieces. What Donizetti's father should have given him was not a scraper but a pair of scissors.

Donizetti, born at Bergamo in 1798, was but seventeen years of age when he commenced his studies in his native town under Mayer, who, before the appearance of Rossini, was one of the most popular composers in Italy; and he finished them (so far as studies can ever be finished) at Bologna under Pilotti and Mattei, the latter of whom had some years previously been Rossini's instructor. Finding that Mattei gave him very few lessons at the Bologna Lyceum, where he was professor, the youthful and ingenious Donizetti contrived to obtain supplementary ones by making himself very agreeable to his master and by turning the conversation as often as possible to musical subjects. He even went so far as to play at cards every evening with Mattei's aged mother, a piece of benevolence for which he was rewarded by much instructive talk from the grateful son. While at the Lyceum Donizetti occupied himself not only with music, but also with drawing, architecture, and even poetry; and that he could turn out fair enough verses for musical purposes was shown when, many years afterwards, he wrote—so rapidly that the word "improvised" might here be used—for the benefit of a manager in distress, both words and music of a little one-act opera, called Il Campanello, founded on the Sonnette de Nuit of Scribe.

No composer, with the exception of Mozart, possessed a more remarkable memory than Donizetti. After two hearings of Allegri's Miserere, Mozart remembered the whole work so as to be able to write it out note for note; and Donizetti, wishing to procure for Mayer a copy of an opera which was being performed at Bologna, and which the impresario had refused to lend, had such a lively recollection of the music after hearing it two or three times that he was able to put it down on paper from beginning to end. Unfortunately the tellers of these stories omit as a rule to say whether the possessors of such wonderful mnemonic powers make notes while hearing the compositions, which, in rather a literal sense, they propose to carry away with them. A prodigious memory for small things as for great would be necessary to enable a musician in the present day to write out, even after a dozen hearings, an opera by Meyerbeer or by Wagner with all the changes of harmony, all the details of instrumentation. The operas, however, of Donizetti's youth were much simpler affairs than these latter-day productions.

Already known by many pieces of instrumental and religious music, Donizetti produced his first opera, Enrico di Borgogna, at Venice in 1818. This work obtained so much success that the composer was requested to undertake at once a second one for the same city. After writing an opera for Mantua in 1819, Il Falignamo di Livonia, Donizetti visited Rome, where his Zoraïde di Granata procured him an exemption from military service, which would otherwise have carried him off, and the honour of being crowned at the Capitol. He now produced a whole series of operas which owed their success chiefly to the skill with which he imitated the style of Rossini. Strangely enough it was not until Rossini had ceased to write that Donizetti, his immediate successor, exhibited something like a style of his own. In 1830, however, the in many parts highly-dramatic Anna Bolena was produced; a work which was long regarded as its composer's masterpiece. Donizetti wrote Anna Bolena for Pasta and Rubini, and it was first represented for Pasta's benefit in the year 1831. In the tenor air, Vivi tu, Rubini made a striking success; and it was in this opera, as Henry VIII., that Lablache first gained the favour of the London public. Anna Bolena was destined soon to be eclipsed by other works from the pen of the same composer; and it is now but rarely, if ever, heard. Many years, indeed, have passed since it was last performed in London with Mdlle. Titiens in the principal character. It contains an unusually large number of expressive, singable melodies; and many of its scenes possess more dramatic significance than belong as a rule to Rossini's Italian works. It marks a step in fact, in the movement from the style of Rossini, as exhibited in his Italian operas, towards that of Verdi; a movement in which Bellini, standing by himself, cannot be said to have had any part. Neither in his earlier operas does Bellini, like Donizetti, resemble Rossini, nor in his later ones does he, like Donizetti, approach what was afterwards to be known as the style of Verdi.

Lucrezia Borgia, written for Milan in 1834, was a distinct advance on Anna Bolena. This work, with Lucia and La Favorita, by which it was to be succeeded, must be ranked among Donizetti's most successful productions; and it has already been pointed out that the three operas just named are the only ones by which Donizetti is now represented regularly every year at our great lyrical theatres. Lucrezia Borgia is based on one of Victor Hugo's most dramatic plays; but the composer has not turned to so effective account as might have been expected, the great scene in which Maffio Orsini's drinking song is interrupted by the funeral dirge given to the procession of monks in the outside street. Like Verdi, some years afterwards, in Ernani and in Rigoletto, Donizetti counted too much on a musical effect which is naturally much more impressive in a spoken drama, where music, until this one scene, has not been heard, than in an opera which is sung throughout. Francis I.'s song, in the drama of Le Roi s'amuse, arrests the attention much more than does the Duke of Mantua's canzone in Rigoletto. The horn of Hernani is mysterious and terrifying in the play, while in the opera, heard after many other horns, not to speak of cornets, trombones, ophecleides, and all the instruments of the Sax family, it scarcely excites even a feeling of surprise. As regards Lucrezia Borgia, though the singers of the drinking-song and the chanters of the burial service have the scene entirely to themselves, yet the contrast between reckless life and inevitable death is less striking in a work where music possesses no special significance than in one where music has been introduced for the sake of impressiveness in the single scene where it is employed. Taking it, however, for what it is worth, Donizetti's successor, Verdi, would doubtless have made more of it than Donizetti himself has done. Maffio Orsini's brindisi is spirited, and characteristically voluptuous. But there is nothing very awe-inspiring in the chorus of monks at the back of the stage; and the two pieces bear no relation to one another—which they might perhaps with advantage have been made to do.

Lucrezia Borgia contains less recitative than belongs to the operas of Rossini, who himself dispensed with the endless monologues and recitatives cultivated by his predecessors. Indeed, the amount of measured talk in Lucrezia Borgia scarcely exceeds that which is to be met with in the most popular of Verdi's works. The brilliancy of the introduction, the series of dramatic scenes—for which the composer had, above all, to thank his librettist, who, in his turn, was indebted to Victor Hugo—and an unusually large number of tuneful themes for four leading personages among whom the interest is judiciously distributed, could not fail to secure for Lucrezia Borgia the success it in fact obtained.

The graceful Elisir d'Amore, which, owing to the prevailing taste for spectacular opera, is now but rarely heard, was given for the first time at Milan in 1832. Donizetti was now composing operas at the rate of about three a year. Many of them made but little impression and scarcely a twelfth part of them are performed in the present day.

In 1835, however, Donizetti produced an opera which was received with enthusiasm, which soon became popular throughout Europe, and which seems to possess as much vitality now as when it was first brought out. Lucia di Lammermoor, the work in question, contains some of the most beautiful melodies, in the sentimental style, that Donizetti has composed; and it is especially admired by musicians for the broadly conceived, well-constructed and highly dramatic finale which brings the second act to so effective a conclusion. The sudden appearance of Edgar of Ravenswood just as his devoted but despairing Lucy has been forced to sign the contract which gives her to another, is but the first of a series of situations, skilfully varied and contrasted, which the librettist has ably planned, and which have been admirably treated by the composer. The part of Lucia, beloved by every "light soprano" of the present day, was written for Persiani; that of Edgardo, which, in the days of the great tenors, was even more popular than the prima donna's part, for Duprez. Of the last act of Lucia, which, until the reign of the light sopranos set in, used to be considered the crowning glory of the opera, Donizetti wrote both words and music. It has already been mentioned that he once transformed a French vaudeville into an Italian opera or operetta; and it may be added that the libretti of Betly and of La Figlia del Reggimento are both from his pen. La Figlia del Reggimento, however, was only La Fille du Régiment translated into Italian; and the libretto of Betly is based, scene by scene, on Adolphe Adam's little opera of Le Chalet—known in English as the Swiss Cottage. In the case of the last act of Lucia, Donizetti not only wrote the words; he designed the scenes. In the novel Edgar loses himself on the seashore, and is drowned. In the opera, however, when so far as Lucia is concerned the story is at an end, he reappears in an appropriate cemetery to celebrate, in a lyrical lament, the virtues of his demented love; to be informed by a chorus of retainers that she has not only lost her reason, but has departed altogether from this world; and finally to stab himself while still singing the praises of his "bell' alma adorata." When the Lucia of the evening is Patti, Nilsson, or Albani, and the Edgardo is no one in particular, the final scene of course falls flat; no one, indeed, stops to hear it. But the case was quite different when the part of Edgardo was filled by a great dramatic vocalist, like Duprez, or in later days by Mario.

In 1835 Donizetti visited Paris, and there brought out his Marino Faliero, remembered for a time by several pretty pieces, including, in particular, the opening chorus for the workmen in the arsenal, and a chorus of gondoliers at the beginning of the second act. He was more successful when revisiting the French capital, in 1840, he produced there his opera of I Martiri, founded on the subject of Polyeucte which, composed for Naples with a view to Nourrit in the principal part, had been objected to by the Neapolitan censorship; La Fille du Régiment, written for and performed at the Opéra Comique; and La Favorite composed in the first instance for a house of the second rank, the Théâtre de la Renaissance, but afterwards transferred to the Académie. La Favorite—or La Favorita, as it became after passing from the French to the Italian stage—has, like Lucrezia Borgia, the advantage of being founded on a highly dramatic story. It is based on a French drama known, until the opera caused it to be forgotten, as Le Comte de Comminges; and it seems to owe its origin to a Spanish work. In La Favorita, as in most Spanish plays, there is no unfolding of the plot through introductory narrative. The action, from the beginning, takes place beneath the eyes of the spectator. A young man, already tired of the world, is seeking repose in the seclusion of a monastery. But he has been troubled by a vision. The vision still haunts him, and the prior vainly exhorts him in a duet to abandon all thought of the external, and to concentrate his attention on the inward and spiritual. Fernando's adventures with the beautiful lady who turns out to be the "favourite" of the king, the recompense bestowed upon him in the shape of this lady's hand for the valour he has shown in the king's service, and his ultimate return to the monastery when he finds how bitterly he has been deceived, need not here be recounted. It is worth observing, however, that the success of the opera has been in a great measure due to the excellence of the libretto; and that in all really good libretti, as in that of La Favorita, the action of the piece, instead of being related, is presented continuously on the stage. The duet of the first act for Fernando and the chief of the monastery is sufficiently interesting. The choruses of women and the ballet music (of which these choruses form part), in the second act, are graceful and melodious; and the king's air in the third act, Pour tant d'amour, has been always liked both by the popular baritones who sing it and by the public. Leonora's scena, too, "O mon Fernand," possesses, at least in the slow movement (the quick one being quite unworthy of it), a certain amount of beauty. But the fourth act of La Favorita is worth all the rest of the opera, and it may well be regarded as the finest act Donizetti has composed. The calmness and purity of the tenor's air, "Ange si pur," and the passionate impulsiveness of the final duet for the despondent lovers, are eminently dramatic: the character of each piece being perfectly in accord with the situation. The choruses are highly impressive, and the whole scene becomes filled with earnest animation as it moves towards the final climax. Donizetti is said to have sketched and in the main to have completed this act at a single sitting, and in the space of some three or four hours. The andante, however, of the duet was added at the rehearsals; and the cavatina, "Ange si pur" was borrowed from the score of a work never brought out—Le Duc d'Albe. If there could be any doubt about the fact, it would be difficult to believe that Fernando's air had not been inspired by the situation in which it occurs. So, after all, in a measure it was; since the composer took it from elsewhere to introduce it where he knew it would be in place.

La Favorita was by no means Donizetti's last work. He had yet to write Linda di Chamouni, in which there is more of what is called "local colour" than in any other of his operas; and Don Pasquale, which, apart from the brightness and gaiety of its never-ending series of melodies, would be remembered if only from the circumstance of its having been written for that incomparable quartet, Grisi, Mario, Tamburini, and Lablache. The very year (1843) that Donizetti produced Don Pasquale at Paris he brought out Maria di Rohan at Vienna. The music of

Maria di Rohan is in some respects the most dramatic that Donizetti has written. The libretto, like almost every good libretto, is based on a French play—Un Duel sous Richelieu; and it contains a very strong part for the baritone, in which, at our Royal Italian Opera, Ronconi has often shown the highest histrionic genius, together with a certain inability to sing in tune. Maria di Rohan, however, is not to be called dramatic simply because it contains one great dramatic part. What is more important is the fact that the music of the work is appropriate to the various personages and to the great situations of the piece. In portraying the original of the jealous husband, Donizetti exhibits all the earnestness and vigour of Verdi, whom, as before observed, he resembles more in Maria di Rohan than in any of his earlier works.

Donizetti's last opera was Catarina Cornaro, brought out at Naples in 1844. This was his sixty-third dramatic work, without counting a certain number—variously estimated, but not likely to be great—which have not been represented. At least two-thirds of Donizetti's operas have never been heard in England. Soon after the production of Catarina Cornaro Donizetti fell into a melancholy condition. Symptoms of dementia manifested themselves while he was on a visit to Paris. The doctors thought the air of his native town might have some salutary effect, and the patient was accordingly ordered to Bergamo; but the case was already a hopeless one. He was taken to Bergamo, but was attacked with paralysis on the journey; and soon after his arrival, having experienced a second attack, he succumbed.

Donizetti, as has already been said, worked for some time before and for many years after Bellini, whom he preceded and survived. Bellini was born in 1806, nine years after Donizetti, and died in 1837, thirteen years before him. He was a native of Sicily, and his father, with whom he took his first lessons in music, was an organist at Catania. The organist was persuaded to send his son to Naples by a Sicilian nobleman, who promised to pay his expenses as a student at the famous Conservatorio, which he in due time entered, and where he had for fellow-pupil Mercadante—more or less known whereever Italian opera has been cultivated by his Giuramento, the only one of his numerous works which ever met with anything like an enduring success. Mercadante was a better musician than Bellini. But he possessed far less creative power; and his creations or inspirations in the shape of melodies are seldom comparable in beauty to those of which the scores of La Sonnambula, Norma, and I Puritani are so full. The tenor's love-song in Il Giuramento, and the highly dramatic duet which brings that opera to a conclusion, will be remembered by all who have once heard this masterpiece of a composer who did not produce masterpieces. Opera-goers of the last thirty years cannot altogether forget him; and it may in particular be observed that he made a far more effective use of the orchestra than his more divinely endowed fellow-student, who thought and felt in melody as Ovid, and afterwards Pope, "lisped in numbers:" every sequence of notes that occurred to him being melodious.

Bellini composed his first work while he was studying at the Conservatorio, where it was afterwards performed. His next production was intended for the outside public. It was entitled Adelson e Salvino, and had the honour, or at least the advantage, of being represented in the presence of the illustrious

Barbaja, who, without being a musician, was, as we have already seen, a keen appreciator of musical excellence. It would have been necessary, perhaps, to have been a little blind not to perceive the merit of three such masters as Rossini, Donizetti, and Bellini. Such blindness however, was as a matter of fact exhibited by a good many, whereas the ex-waiter of the San Carlo gambling saloon showed himself clear-sighted in the matter. Rossini and Donizetti had both been under engagements to Barbaja, and he was not going to allow Bellini to escape him. The famous impresario was at this time director of the San Carlo at Naples, of the Scala at Milan, of some smaller operatic establishments in Italy, and of the Italian Opera at Vienna. He commissioned Bellini in the first place to write an opera for Naples, where, in 1826, he brought out his Bianca e Fernando. This work obtained no very great amount of success. But it pleased a considerable portion of the public; and it so far satisfied Barbaja that the sagacious manager entrusted the young composer, now twenty years of age, with the libretto of Il Pirata, in which the principal part was to be written specially for Rubini. This time Bellini's opera was to be produced at La Scala. In the simple touching melodies of Il Pirata—of which the principal one for the tenor, quickly laid hold of by composers for the pianoforte and the violin, was still remembered long after the opera, as a whole, had been forgotten—Bellini at once revealed the character of his genius; and the composer of twenty was destined to express the reaction he felt within himself, and which the public was prepared to feel, against the florid style of Rossini. While composing Il Pirata, Bellini retired into the country with the singer on whose execution the success of the work would so much depend. Rubini sang the melodies of his part as Bellini wrote them; and Bellini is said not to have succeeded all at once in inducing him to abandon his taste for ornamentation, and in prevailing upon him to deliver the simple phrases of his principal airs, not only from the chest, but also from the heart. Rubini and his composer, Bellini and his singer, soon understood one another; and in his great scene the admired tenor excited the utmost enthusiasm. Now were fulfilled the words of the prophet Stendhal (or perhaps it was the seer Carpani beneath whose mantle Stendhal, we know, was in the habit of concealing himself), who, writing only some two or three years before, had foretold that Rossini would be followed by a composer remarkable for the simplicity of his style.

After producing in succession La Straniera (Milan, 1828), Zaira (Parma, 1829), Bellini brought out at Venice his operatic version of Romeo and Juliet, under the title of I Capuletti ed i Montecchi which owed such success as it obtained to the singing of Mdle. Pasta, as Il Pirata had been indebted for the favour with which it was received to the singing of Rubini. The years 1829, 1830, 1831, and 1832 are especially memorable in the history of Italian opera; for in the first of these Rossini's William Tell, in the second Donizetti's Anna Bolena, in the third Bellini's Sonnambula, and in the fourth Bellini's Norma, was produced. The Italian school of operatic music was certainly at that time supreme in Europe; and Rossini, Donizetti, and Bellini continued for many years to hold sway at theatres where they have now to share their dominion with the composers of France and Germany—with Gounod, Ambroise Thomas, and Bizet, with Meyerbeer and with Wagner.

La Sonnambula, as the work of a new composer, was a good

deal sneered at on the occasion of its first production in London. But its endless flow of melodies—many of which, being full of true emotion, are so far thoroughly dramatic—could not fail to ensure its success, with the public at large; and this success, now of half a century's duration, has scarcely diminished since the part of Amina was first undertaken by Pasta, and that of Elvino by Rubini. Our old friend, Lord Mount-Edgcumbe, true type of the praiser of times gone by, having been scared by Rossini, was not likely to be calmed down by Bellini. Of Norma he tells us that the scene of the opera was laid "in Wales," and that it "was not liked." It is difficult to understand the mood of one, having ears to hear, who, whatever he might think of Norma as a specimen of the highest kind of tragic opera, could fail to "like it." Rossini, together with a mass of opera-goers in all countries, was of those who not only "liked" but greatly admired Norma; and he gave the composer the benefit of his counsels when the still young Bellini (he was even now only thirty years of age) undertook to write an opera for the Italian Theatre of Paris, with Grisi, Rubini, Tamburini, and Lablache in the principal parts. The effect of Rossini's advice may be seen in the greater degree of attention paid by Bellini to the orchestration of I Puritani and to the concerted music. It would have been well if some one had recommended Bellini not to set to work upon so poor a libretto as that of I Puritani derived from Ancelot's poor novel, Les Puritains d'Ecosse. Rubini's air, "Ah te, o cara," the polacca for Grisi, the duet in three movements for Tamburini and Lablache,—as to which Rossini, writing an account of the opera to a friend at Milan, remarked that some echo of the final outburst for the two voices, with its brazen accompaniments, must surely have reached him,—and the beautiful tenor solo of the closing concerted piece: these in themselves must have been enough to secure the success of the opera. The last-named melody for the tenor voice, so thoroughly religious in character, was sung at Bellini's funeral to the words of the Lacrymosa; and it was in the midst of the enthusiasm created by his last work that Bellini, at the age of thirty-eight, died.

CHAPTER XIII

VERDI

GUISEPPE VERDI, the successor at once of Bellini and of Donizetti, but whose energetic style bears a far greater resemblance to that of Donizetti in his later works (Maria di Rohan, for instance) than to that of Bellini, was born near Parma, on the 9th of October, 1814. His father was an innkeeper in a humble way of business, and Verdi's first lessons in music were taken from the local organist. In 1833, thanks to the assistance of a rich patron of art, he went to Milan, where for three years he studied under Lavigna, musical conductor at the Scala Theatre. It was not until 1839 that he succeeded in getting his first opera, Oberto, Conte di San Bonifazio, produced. But the manager of the Scala, where it was performed was so satisfied with its success that he gave the young composer an order for three other works. Unfortunately at this juncture Verdi lost a wife whom he had recently married and to whom he was tenderly attached. He had just undertaken the uncongenial and now hateful task of composing an opera buffa entitled, Un Giorno di Regno; and, as might have been expected, this work was somewhat deficient in comedy. It failed; and so complete was the fiasco that the director of La Scala felt himself justified in declining to receive from Verdi the two other operas which he had agreed to take.

The unhappy composer had now to begin his career again; and

as the first step he passed a year without writing a note. He then set to work once more and composed his well-known opera on the subject of Nebuchadnezzar, called familiarly Nabuco. Nabucodonosore, produced in London, where the biblical subject had been objected to by the censorship, under the title of Nino, was the first work by which Verdi became famous out of his own country; and the success of Nabuco became in due time European. Nabuco (1842) was followed by I Lombardi (1843), and Ernani (1844); and the three works by which Verdi established his reputation in Italy were all given without much delay at Her Majesty's Theatre. The first production, in fact, of Verdi's works dates from immediately before the secession which led to the establishment of the Royal Italian Opera. An opera on the subject of the Two Foscari was brought out at Rome in 1844, and some three or four years afterwards was given at the Royal Italian Opera, with Ronconi in the principal part. Ernani, however, at both our rival opera houses was for some time the most admired and the most often played of the new composer's works.

At this time Verdi's music met with but little appreciation from critics, who declared it to be noisy and commonplace, and who were particularly offended by so much brass being employed in the orchestration, and by so many of the choruses being written in unison. The new composer was accused, moreover, of passing too abruptly from one piece to another, of not sufficiently preparing his effects, and so on. We have seen how Rossini was attacked when his operas were first produced in England; and the Lord Mount-Edgcumbes of 1848, and indeed of many years later, were thoroughly dissatisfied with Verdi, whom it was the fashion to represent in the newspapers of the day as a sort of melodramatic mountebank. Even as late as 1856, when the richly melodious, and in many respects highly dramatic Trovatore was given at the Royal Italian Opera, the talent, or rather the genius of Verdi, was still systematically denied. The style in which Verdi's operas were habitually executed in London may have had something to do with the charges pressed so energetically against him. Those, however, who have heard Verdi conduct his own works are aware that though his scores may contain parts for a considerable number of brass instruments, yet the brassiness of the orchestra is kept down and a proper balance of sonority maintained. Fully informed as to why Verdi's works ought not to be admired, the public of London persisted in admiring them; and it may be here mentioned that for some years Verdi was not much better treated by the critical press of France than by that of England. M. Scudo, writing in the Revue des deux Mondes found in Verdi the same faults already mentioned as those of which he was habitually accused in England. Il Trovatore, however, did much towards converting M. Scudo; and the success of that work, if not the work itself, did much to shake the faith, or rather the unfaith, of those English critics and connoisseurs who had previously disbelieved in Verdi. The production of Rigoletto at the Royal Italian Opera a year or two later, with Madame Bosio (most charming of Gildas), Signor Mario, and Signor Ronconi in the principal parts, made those who were still sceptical as to Verdi's high merits appear somewhat ridiculous. La Traviata, with its questionable story derived from the younger Dumas's novel and play of La Dame aux Camélias, was a good deal blamed by reason of its libretto; and also on account of the alleged triviality of the music, which, however, thanks to the tone of genuine emotion in many of its strains, still lives, and is now, indeed, more popular than ever.

Verdi's success in England was confirmed, and more than confirmed, by the production at the Royal Italian Opera of Un Ballo in Maschera (founded on the same subject as Auber's Gustave III.), with an execution which was above all remarkable for the style in which the part of the Duke, vaguely described as "Il Duca," was played by Signor Mario, and that of Renato, whose wife the Duke betrays, by Signor Graziani; and for the last twelve or fifteen years it has been considered bad taste not to admire Verdi's music. Indeed, since Aïda, his latest, most serious, most studied, and, in the true sense of the word, most dramatic opera, it has become the fashion in some musical circles to place him above all other Italian composers, to contrast the significance of his melodies, the characterisation of his personages, and the forcible construction of his scenes, with the careless, haphazard stringing together of meaningless, if singable tunes, and of ingenious rather than dramatic concerted pieces which mark the style or want of style of so many Italian composers. It is only fair, however, to remember that Verdi has not yet surpassed William Tell, that he has produced nothing superior in the way of concerted finale to the celebrated one which closes the second act of Lucia, and that he scarcely could have treated the last act of La Favorita more dramatically, or with a greater abundance of melodic ideas than Donizetti—here by the way, writing at times very much in Verdi's own manner.

In pursuing the story of Verdi's constantly increasing success among the English we have departed from the general history of his career. It must be mentioned, however, that many of Verdi's operas which gained great favour in Italy have either never been given in England at all, or have been performed in this country without exciting much enthusiasm. Nor was any great impression made in England by the work which, under the title of Masnadieri, Verdi wrote expressly for Her Majesty's Theatre in the days of Jenny Lind, with Jenny Lind herself, Gardoni, and Lablache in the principal parts. No one seems to have suggested that Verdi's King Lear should be performed in England; but from time to time there has been some talk of producing his Macbeth, of which a French version was brought out, not unsuccessfully, at the Théâtre Lyrique of Paris, with some additional music, and especially some new ballet scenes by the composer.

It is scarcely worth while to recall Verdi's failures: but Luisa Miller and La Forza del Destino must in fairness be reckoned among the number. Luisa Miller is based on the theme of Schiller's pathetic but over-dolorous drama Cabale und Liebe. For the basis of La Forza Verdi did not have recourse to Schiller as in the case of Luisa Miller and I Massdieri, nor to Victor Hugo as in that of Ernani and of Rigoletto (Le Roi s'amuse). His librettist borrowed the subject from a most sanguinary melodrama by a Spanish author of some distinction, though with such bloodthirsty tendencies that he brings almost every character in his play to a violent end, while one of the leading personages, after apparently meeting his death, is restored to life to be killed again. In La Forza del Destino the composer has so neglected the concerted music that the work does not include one regularly constructed concerted piece. It contains, however, some beautiful melodies for the solo voice, including one in particular assigned to the prima donna, which Verdi, from having inscribed it beneath one of his best portraits, would seem to regard as characteristically his own. Of Verdi's Requiem, composed in memory of Manzoni, little need be said except that it is melodious, impressive, and often very dramatic—dramatic, however, in the style of Aïda not of the less thoroughly dramatic, but more stagey works of Verdi's youth.

Verdi, now (1880) in his sixty-seventh year, has by no means renounced musical composition; and he is understood to be actively engaged on a new Othello, of which Signor Boito, author and composer of Mefistofele, has furnished the libretto, and which is to be brought out as soon as completed under the title of Iago.

Unlike other composers, Verdi has played a certain political part, which, however, seems in a great measure to have been forced upon him. In the days before Italian unity it was discovered that the letters composing his name might, in due order, be regarded as signifying "Vittore Emanuele, Re d'Italia"; so that "Viva Verdi!" came to be accepted as an aspiration for a united Italian kingdom with Victor Emanuel on the throne. When Macbeth was brought out, all sorts of political allusions were discovered in the libretto; and nothing would satisfy the electors of Verdi's native town but to make him a member of the National Assembly of Parma. After the formation of the Italian kingdom Verdi became a member of the Italian parliament; and in 1874 the king made him a senator.

LIST OF ROSSINI'S WORKS

WITH THE DATE OF THEIR PRODUCTION IN PUBLIC

1. Il Pianto d'Armonia. Cantata, 1808

2. Orchestral Symphony. 1809

3. Quartet for Stringed Instruments. 1809

4. La Cambiale di Matrimonio. Opera, 1810

5. L'Equivoco Stravagante. Opera, 1811

6. Didone Abbandonata. Cantata, 1811

7. Demetrio e Polibio. Opera, 1811

8. L'Inganno Felice. Opera, 1812

9. Ciro in Babilonia. Opera, 1812

10. La Scala di Seta. Opera, 1812

11. La Pietra del Paragone. Opera, 1812

12. L'Occasione fa il Ladro. Opera, 1812

13. Il Figlio per Azzardo. Opera, 1813

14. Tancredi. Opera, 1813

15.   L'Italiana in Algeri. Opera, 1813

16.   L'Aureliano in Palmira. Opera, 1814

17.   Egle e Irene. Cantata (unpublished), 1814

18.   Il Turco in Italia. Opera, 1814

19.   Sigismondo. Opera, 1814

20.   Elisabetta. Opera, 1815

21.   Torvaldo e Dorliska. Opera, 1816

22.   Il Barbiere di Seviglia. Opera, 1816

23.   La Gazella. Opera, 1816

24.   Otello. Opera, 1816

25.   Teti e Peleo. Cantata, 1816

26.   Cenerentola. Opera, 1817

27.   La Gazza Ladra. Opera, 1817

28.   Armida. Opera, 1817

29.   Adelaida di Borgagna. Opera, 1818

30.   Mosè Opera, 1818

31.   Adina. Opera (written for Lisbon), 1818

32.   Ricciardo e Zoraïde. Opera, 1818

33.   Ermoine. Opera, 1819

34.   Eduardo e Cristina. Opera, 1819

35.   La Donna del Lago. Opera, 1819

36.   Cantata in honour of the King of Naples. 1819

37.   Bianca e Faliero. Opera, 1820

38.   Maometto II. Opera, 1820

39.   Cantata in honour of the Emperor of Austria. 1820

40.   Matilda di Shubrun. Opera, 1821

41.   La Riconoscenza. Cantata, 1821

42.   Zelmira. Opera, 1822

43.   Il vero Omaggio. Cantata, 1822

44.   Semiramide. Opera, 1823

45.   Il Viaggio a Reims. Opera, 1825

46.   Le Siège de Corinthe. Opera, 1826

47.   Moïse. Opera, 1827

48.   Le Comte Ory. Opera, 1828

49.   Guillaume Tell. Opera, 1829

50.   Les Soirées musicales. Douze morceaux de Chant, 1840

51.   Quatre Ariettes Italiennes. 1841

52.   Stabat Mater. 1842

THE END